# THE CLARINET TEACHER'S COMPANION

"Private Lessons on the Clarionet" by F. H. Townsend
(*Cassell's Magazine*, 1890)

# The Clarinet
# Teacher's Companion

PAMELA WESTON

LONDON
ROBERT HALE & COMPANY

*Distributed to the Music Trade by*
Breitkopf & Härtel (London) Ltd.,
for Fenette Music

© *Pamela Weston 1976*

*First published in Great Britain 1976*

ISBN 0 7091 5482 8

Robert Hale & Company
Clerkenwell House
Clerkenwell Green
London EC1R 0HT

PRINTED IN GREAT BRITAIN BY
CLARKE, DOBLE & BRENDON LTD.
PLYMOUTH

# CONTENTS

# PREFACE

The clarinet teacher has a wealth of technical manuals from which to select the one most suited to his own particular line of approach. But in general these are written from the standpoint of the student and not of the teacher, so that the teacher must search the corners of his memory for the way in which he had the steps set before him and the way in which he was shown how to overcome technical difficulties. The teacher needs reading matter for himself which will enable him to deliver the goods clearly and confidently to the pupil. More, he needs information on allied subjects such as history and psychology, to fill in the background and broaden his total understanding. It is with these needs in mind that I have written *The Clarinet Teacher's Companion*. The book does not intend to supplant the chosen manual but rather to supplement it.

Teaching cannot be done without experience. Before one has experience oneself one must draw on the experience of others, and so a knowledge of the working methods of great teachers of the past is an essential to the teacher of today. For this reason the *Companion* begins with a chapter on the history of clarinet teaching, and throughout the book quotations from past methods are used to amplify statements made. Nowhere is the past more important than in the use of ornaments and so in the chapter on this subject I have drawn extensively from a clarinet tutor of the Baroque period for illustration.

The psychology of teaching, of learning, of performance and nerves, all so important, are severally considered. Practising is given a chapter to itself and so is the selection, treatment and repairs of equipment.

The main portion of the *Companion* deals with the teaching of technique. Here a complete programme is given in chapters on basic method, breathing, embouchure, tone, intonation, tonguing, finger work, rhythm, interpretation, sight reading and transposition. Each subject is described, ways of presentation suggested, faults of production enumerated, etc.

I would like to record the inspiration and debt I owe to my own teacher Frederick Thurston who died in 1953. My warmest thanks go to Margaret Leonard and Shirley Jeremy for reading the manuscript and offering helpful suggestions, and to Messrs Cassell for permission to reproduce "Private Lessons on the Clarionet" as the frontispiece.

PAMELA WESTON

London, 1975

# NOTES

The fingerings used in this book are for the standard Boehm clarinet of 17 keys and 6 rings.

The following method of describing the fingers is used:

First finger—'index',
Second finger—'middle',
Third finger—'ring',
Fourth finger—'little'.

The following system of notation is used:

Notes below middle C—e, f, etc.,
From middle C upwards—c', d', etc.,
From the next octave—c", d", etc.,
From the final octave—c''', d''', etc.

# 1

# A Short History of Clarinet Teachers and their Methods

The names of Lefèvre, Klosé and Carl Baermann have become bywords in the world of clarinet teaching because the tutors they wrote, during the first half of the nineteenth century, were so well founded that they are still being printed for use today. All three men also took a hand in the improvement of the instrument, particularly Klosé. They were not alone in what they did and were influenced by other performers, teachers and inventors, so that to understand the value of their contributions this history must include also the following : Beer and Tausch, the early virtuosi who were responsible for the emergence of style in clarinet playing; Müller, the intrepid much-travelling performer who invented the Simple system instrument; and Berr, professor at the Paris Conservatoire, who brought many reforms into teaching and laid the foundation of present-day technique.

## BEER AND TAUSCH

Joseph Beer (1744–1812) and Franz Tausch (1762–1817) were the first important performers on the clarinet and were each responsible for developing a distinctive style of playing. They were also the first teachers of note and though neither man wrote a tutor their influence through their pupils was profound. Beer's style, which became known as the 'French' because of his lengthy sojourn in France at the outset of his career, was fluent and technically brilliant but with a tone that was powerful and strident. Tausch, whose style was known as the 'German', put beauty of tone and detail of expression foremost, whilst at the same time he also achieved great technical mastery.

Beer, during his early years in Paris, taught Etienne Solère and Michel Yost, who both became notable performers. He left Paris in middle age and while travelling through Germany was so impressed by the style of playing he found there that he immediately set about mellowing his own tone and developing a more expressive delivery. He travelled on to Russia and his superlative playing earned him many highly successful years there. His final years were spent as chamber musician to the King of Prussia, who appointed him teacher at the School of Military Music in Potsdam. Tausch held appointments at the courts of Mannheim, Munich and Berlin. At the latter he shared the playing at court with Beer, and in 1805 founded a Conservatoire for Wind Players where he trained many first-rate players. In its opening year Heinrich Baermann became a pupil. As he had previously learnt from Beer at Potsdam, Beer and Tausch can claim to be jointly responsible for forming one of the greatest clarinettists the world has ever known. Finland's Crusell was another well-known player to imbibe qualities from both German and French styles, for he had lessons first from Tausch and then from Yost's pupil Lefèvre.

### LEFÈVRE

Jean Xavier Lefèvre (1763–1829) lived in Paris throughout the turbulent years of the French Revolution and the Napoleonic wars. His playing was dazzling, after the original French style of Beer. Besides being a notable soloist, he held most of the important appointments in the city, including that of first clarinet to the Emperor. Because of the large number of clarinet players required for the military bands in Napoleon's armies there was a big demand for lessons and when the Paris Conservatoire opened its doors in 1795 Lefèvre was one of nineteen professors appointed to teach a hundred and four clarinet pupils. Lefèvre was commissioned to write the official tutor for use in the Conservatoire classes and this was printed by the institute's press in 1802. The tutor was brought out in later editions by Hermann Bender, Romeo Orsi and Alamiro Giampieri. It also formed the basis of Julius Pisařo-vic's method, and is still in use today.

## MÜLLER

Iwan Müller (1786–1854) delivered his thirteen-keyed clarinet to the Paris Conservatoire for them to examine in 1812. He claimed that this new clarinet could play in all keys with ease, so that performers would in future need only one instrument. He was unlucky in having Lefèvre as a member of the committee appointed to judge it, for Lefèvre considered the drilling of more holes than were necessary for his six-keyed clarinet detrimental to the tone of the instrument and undoubtedly influenced the jury. The invention was in fact rejected on the grounds that composers desired the variety of tone colour offered by clarinets of different pitches. Müller refused to be beaten and travelled all over Europe and to Russia giving such brilliant performances on the instrument that it was soon heralded as the clarinet of the future. Müller was a wanderer for most of his life and never settled long enough to make a reputation as a teacher, but he did write a method for his clarinet in 1822 and this went successfully into several later editions.

## BERR AND KLOSÉ

In 1831 Frederic Berr (1794–1838) was appointed professor at the Paris Conservatoire and in his short seven years of office brought about many reforms. He had been an early admirer of Müller's and lost no time in insisting on the adoption of Müller's clarinet by the Conservatoire; he made his pupils change from playing with the reed on top to underneath, and then set about instilling the German ideals of tone into them. In 1836 he wrote a tutor on lines similar to Müller's, but for a fourteen-keyed clarinet. This was reprinted many times and appeared much later in an edition by Prospère Mimart. Berr dedicated the tutor to his pupil Hyacinthe Eléonore Klosé (1808–1880), who took over the professorship when his master died in 1838. Klosé, besides becoming a successful and much-loved teacher, was famous as the inventor, in collaboration with the instrument-maker Louis-Auguste Buffet, of the seventeen-key six-ring Boehm system clarinet. The Boehm, although quite as revolutionary in design as Müller's clarinet, met with no opposition in France and quickly became the popular instrument. Acceptance elsewhere was slower, England not adopting it until near the end of the nineteenth century, but it is now the system most commonly used in all western European countries and in America. Klosé wrote a method for his clarinet in 1843 of which later editions were made by Giampieri, Simeon Bellison and Charles Draper. In 1855 Joseph Williams, the Herefordshire clarinettist, whilst not converted to the Boehm, wrote a tutor embodying Klosé's teaching principles but applying them to a thirteen-keyed instrument which he played with the reed on top.

### CARL BAERMANN

Müller's clarinet, known as the Simple system, became increasingly popular in eastern Europe and Russia where today it is still the system most used. Amongst the permutations of this form of clarinet is a model of eighteen keys designed in 1860 by Carl Baermann (1810–1885), the son of Heinrich Baermann. Carl was a very fine teacher, for many years professor at the Royal Music School in Munich. Between the years 1864 and 1875 he wrote an elaborate and successful method, which later appeared in editions by Oskar Schubert, Gustave Langenus and Bellison. This has been adapted also for the Boehm clarinet.

### EVOLUTION OF TECHNIQUE

#### 1. *Starting Notes and Fingering*

Methods of starting the pupil have varied during the instrument's metamorphosis. Amand Vanderhagen (1753–1822), who in 1785 wrote the first serious tutor, began his pupils on the note c″. He avoided the chalumeau register because these notes were hard to produce well on instruments of that time. By the end of the century manufacturers had improved the low notes considerably and as these were less demanding on the embouchure teachers then adopted g′ or c′ for a starting note. With the advent of the Boehm clarinet g′ and c′ became less good, the former presenting a problem of balance and the latter a problem of difficult finger spacing. Nowadays, to avoid these problems, most teachers choose to start on e′. In the early days it was not considered important to cover the holes with the flat of the finger and illustrations of the time frequently show the fingers in a bent position. But the introduction of ring keys, necessitating the covering of a ring as well as a hole, made it essential to flatten the finger, using the bigger area of the pad instead of the tip. Teachers have agreed, through all stages in the development of technique, that finger action should be vigorous and kept small and precise.

## 2. *Reed Position and Tonguing*

The clarinet was blown with the reed on top for well over its first hundred years of existence. The tongue was used for articulation, but as it could not touch the reed it had only remote control and quick repeated notes were virtually impossible. On hearing this method still being used in the 1880s, a writer described it as sounding like playing on the glottis of a goose. Although in 1782 a Norwegian tutor came out with the idea of playing with the reed underneath, very little notice was taken of it until the indefatigable Müller spoke out strongly in favour of the method. Turning the mouthpiece round enabled the tongue to have direct contact with the reed and it became obvious then that complete control in the starting and stopping of the reed's vibrations was possible. This method is now practically universal, though instances of the older method are still found in Spain and Italy.

## 3. *Embouchure*

The intonation of sounds is controlled by degrees of jaw pressure against the reed. As the upper jaw is static the lower jaw has to apply this pressure, and during the time that the clarinet was played reed uppermost this meant the pressure could not be applied direct but only through the medium of the mouthpiece. The turning round of the mouthpiece, by allowing the lower jaw to come into contact with the reed, meant direct influence on the latter, with great general improvement in control. In the early days embouchure was always 'double lip', that is to say both lips were tucked over the teeth. The teeth could not have been allowed in contact with mouthpieces of the time, for the latter were made of wood and this would have become damaged. Wood was an unsatisfactory medium in other ways too, for it tended to crack and warp, thus ruining the lay. Many experiments were therefore made with other materials and in the 1870s ebonite was found to be a suitable substitute. Now there was no reason to continue the top lip's discomfort when playing with it tucked over the teeth. The lip could be released and the teeth placed on the mouthpiece without damaging it. The lip's function of preventing escape of air could be performed just as well, if not better, in this position. Carl Baermann was one of the first to adopt this 'single lip' embouchure, pointing out that as greater endurance was now possible reliability of tone control was improved enormously.

Few significant changes in clarinet techique occurred during eighty years or so from the time of Baermann's tutor; instead it was a period of consolidation. But since then composers have been exploiting the wind instruments more and more, introducing quarter-tones, chords etc., so that technique has had to expand considerably. The new monophonic and multiphonic possibilities have been expertly and thoroughly set out in *New Sounds for Woodwind* by Bruno Bartolozzi* and this should be on every wind teacher's bookshelf. It is the young to whom new music appeals most easily and the teacher should let them be the ambassadors of the future, keeping himself abreast of contemporary trends with them and adapting his method to keep pace.

* Oxford University Press.

# 2
# *General Observations on Teaching*

## REQUIREMENTS IN A TEACHER

The first requirement in a teacher is that he should have a genuine desire to show and help others, and love doing it. A musician who does not want to teach may turn to doing it if he is unable to break in on the limited performing world. If this is the case, then he should not do it, for he will not succeed. The second requirement is that he should 'practise what he preaches', and this applied to the clarinet teacher means he must not be a *musical factotum*, but a specialist on his own particular instrument. The malpractice of the 'woodwind coach' who attempts to teach instruments as dissimilar as the no-reed flute, the single-reed clarinet, and the double-reed oboe and bassoon cannot be too strongly condemned. The embouchure for each of these three types is so individual that only concentration on the moulding and training of the muscles for *one* particular type can produce a high enough degree of skill for teaching it. It is horrifying to think of the potential virtuosi who have been deprived of their chance in life by being given wrong instruction at the outset, through ignorance on the part of the non-specialist teacher.

The clarinet teacher then is a specialist executant who is drawn to imparting his skill to others. It is necessary that he has at least a modicum of experience in public performance for without this the art of presentation and the difficulties that beset a performer cannot properly be understood. If he does not keep up his performing when he becomes a teacher then he should keep his faculties alive by attending concerts and master classes given by great artists, and have the occasional extra lesson himself. He should broaden his knowledge of other styles of performance and teaching in this way, and thus keep his own method flexible. He must be convinced of the rightness of his method when teaching a beginner, but in taking on a pupil who has been brought up on another method his flexibility will allow him to take the moderate course of integrating the two methods rather than sweeping the alien method overboard.

The teacher must be willing to demonstrate to the pupil and this should be done fairly often during the early lessons, when the pupil forms the strongest impressions. After that, except for playing duets with him, demonstrations might be kept to rare occasions so that the pupil has a chance to develop a style of his own. It is an asset for the clarinet teacher to be a pianist so that he can direct lessons from the piano. This has the following advantages: the teacher can talk at the same time as playing, demonstrate a musical point more promptly, watch the pupil more easily and by accompanying him provide a much fuller musical experience.

## REQUIREMENTS IN A PUPIL

Amongst the qualities that a would-be clarinettist should possess, which Carl Baermann enumerates in his *Vollständige Clarinette-Schule* (Offenbach 1864–1875), are: "Enthusiasm . . . and determination to persevere in perfecting his art to the utmost of his ability." His enthusiasm should be genuinely for the sound of the clarinet, he should be able and quick to respond to teaching, and willing to practise for a definite period each day. Beyond these general qualifications careful consideration should be given to a youthful beginner's general size and physical development. If he is too small to support the instrument's weight of approximately 1 lb. 12 oz. on his right thumb, and if his fingers are not long enough to span the holes, nor his teeth adequately developed, then he should be dissuaded until later. The great Czech teacher František Tadeuš Blatt (1793–1856) says in his *Méthode complète de Clarinette* (Paris 1843) that he considers 11, 12 or at most 13 years is the best starting age, for "then the chest can be strengthened and developed, and the fingers acquire the necessary flexibility". Dentists on the other hand say that no wind instrument should be blown before 13 because it will misshape the mouth. Taking all these points into account I consider it is a mistake to *advise* a child under 11 or 12 to take up the clarinet. But if he has a real unprompted desire to learn, then do not stop him, for successful, very young starts have been made in the past, including Tausch at 6 years old and others at 8. In the case of the mature person who wants to learn, but has perhaps a bad tooth structure or double-jointed fingers, yet let him learn, for there are ways of helping malformed teeth, and playing style can be adapted to unwieldy fingers. After all, the great flautist Albert Fransella managed to play with only one lung. Pupils should not be dissuaded because of a supposed superfluity of clarinet players either; they do not all need to be soloists or orchestral players and can join chamber groups or wind bands, of which there will always be plenty if the instrumental supply is good.

The teacher is often asked whether it is good for a would-be pupil to play a recorder first. The answer is yes, in so far as any musical experience will be good for him. But specifically as an introduction to the clarinet the answer is no, because the recorder is different in its blowing, embouchure, tonguing and fingering. For this reason, if the pupil is already playing the recorder when he takes up the clarinet he should be advised to stop, at least temporarily.

## AMATEURS AND PROFESSIONALS

The ambition of the amateur pupil is no different from that of the would-be professional; both wish to master their instrument to the highest degree, one for love, the other for gain. Both will set their sights high in their own way and so must the teacher or he will betray their trust in him. The teacher who is weak enough not to insist on the practice of technique for all pupils alike is no real teacher, for none of them will attain ease of performance without it.

## TEACHING AIMS

The aim of teaching is to show the best approach by direction and example, then to guide the pupil along the path, preventing him from going astray. Each new point should be put over with tact and firmness, the teacher speaking slowly and not omitting to state the obvious. A good relationship with the pupil throughout is essential and he should be encouraged to talk about his problems, to evaluate his performance and criticize it constructively. Fair comment should always be given him, whether he has done well or ill. Irritation or anger on the part of the teacher at an oft-repeated or outrageous mistake must not occur, for it shocks the pupil, and will not erase the mistake; only a patient searching after the *reason* for the mistake will do this.

## PROCEDURE

Each lesson should include hearing and evaluating what the pupil has practised, the teaching of new material, and revision.

It will begin with long notes which, besides being necessary for exercising the breathing and embouchure muscles, produce composure in the pupil. Then will follow the rest of what the pupil has practised, along the lines of the plan set out in Chapter 13. The teacher needs constantly to bear in mind that the pupil cannot move as fast as himself and must be allowed to take his time. Each piece should be studied beyond the stage of mere notes and rhythm, otherwise the finer points of interpretation are never reached, but the teacher must know when to call a halt and change to other music before staleness sets in. At a later stage the original piece can be revised and then taken to a higher degree of performance. Revision should take place regularly, for it is always enjoyable to pupils and is a great restorer of confidence, especially to the backward ones. In presenting new material the teacher should first mark all breathing places and special fingerings, as far as possible keeping the former above the notes and the latter below. By giving this preliminary help the teacher ensures a correct first approach. If this is not done and the pupil starts off wrongly it will take him twice as long to put it right because of the habits already formed.

## PROBLEMS

The commonest problem a teacher has to face is the pupil who is continually stumbling. This generally means he is not looking ahead and a simple expedient is for the teacher to run a ruler along the line of music as it is being played, covering up as far as a bar ahead. To look ahead brings memory into play and memorizing must form a definite part of the pupil's instruction (see Chapter 14). If a pupil persists in a certain error, even after careful explanation and assistance with practice, then the implication is that he is unaware of what he is doing wrong. Awareness can be brought about in two ways; first, by giving an exaggerated demonstration to him and secondly, by asking him to do *precisely what you have been trying to stop him doing.* Suppose the pupil persists in hurrying a simple passage; ask him to do it again on an *accelerando,* and reinforce this by asking him to play an easy scale also on an *accelerando.* Suppose the error is faulty intonation; ask him to pull the barrel joint out half an inch, then play the passage with him on the piano. Reinforce this too with an easy scale, when he will hear the instrument's out-of-tuneness within itself.

### TENSIONS

The teacher should be on the look out for unnecessary stresses and tensions, and ease them for the pupil. Sometimes there is an obvious over-all tension; this can often be alleviated by making the pupil stop playing, inhale deeply, then exhale to empty the lungs completely and rest a few moments. If the pupil complains that he plays always in a tensed-up condition, then a course of very soft slow practising should be recommended until the tension disappears. There are other less obvious signs of tension such as frowning, harsh tone, a finger held high off the instrument, fingers gripping, fingers banging. These can all be dealt with specifically or they can be dealt with in the more general way indicated before, for they may be a symptom of general rather than local tension.

### CHOICE OF MATERIAL

It goes without saying that the teacher has a duty to give the pupil *good* material in a balanced diet of classical and modern music. Few pupils like every piece a teacher asks them to study. Dislike of a piece means lack of appreciation of the music or, more often, lack of ideas for practising. If demonstration of the piece by the teacher or suggestion of new ways of practising do not produce a greater liking, it should be discarded in favour of something else. Occasionally the pupil is met with who loves his clarinet but appears bored by all music given him. Probing is likely to discover that the composer of the music which originally attracted him to the clarinet, or a composer who is 'with it' but has not yet been on the agenda, is what appeals. The favoured composer is then given *ad nauseum*, even if it means using arrangements. After satiation, emancipation is gained and the pupil becomes quite ready to play anything that is put before him! (I had this experience with a girl whose 'love' was Debussy. After treatment of Debussy in every conceivable form she really enjoyed everything.)

# 3
# *Equipment*

Before the pupil comes for his first lesson the teacher should enquire about his instrument. If he already has one but this is not in good order then it must be put right before starting, otherwise frustration will spoil his initial efforts. On the other hand if he has one which is unsuitable then this must be exchanged. In the case of the latter or if he has not one at all then the teacher should give advice and arrange to select one for him. Apart from good tone quality the most important consideration in choosing an instrument is that its mechanism should be sound. For this reason it is better for the pupil to have a new clarinet, even if this has to be cheap or even hired, rather than a second hand one. The cheaper varieties of clarinet are now usually made of plastic. This has certain advantages, notably that it is more durable and that the pitch is less affected by temperature changes than wood. Wood is used for all the more expensive instruments as it gives the better tone quality. One further point to be considered is that at a later stage the pupil will need an A clarinet, which should preferably be of the same make and model as his Bb. This means that if the pupil chooses first one of the cheaper models which is only made in Bb, then he will have to sell it later and buy a pair. In view of this the pupil who is destined for the profession should buy a good quality pair of wood clarinets at the start, and not have to change later on.

No two clarinets of the same make and model are alike, even though they are mass-produced, and when the teacher goes to select he should make sure he is given a fair number to test. All the mechanism must be thoroughly tried out, the keys examined for good venting and springing, and quality of tone and intonation assessed. If the instrument is of wood then it must be closely examined for cracks on the outside or roughness inside the bore. When the choice has to be made from second-hand instruments the testing must be more stringent and any alterations made by previous owners discovered and carefully considered before buying.

### SELECTION OF MOUTHPIECE AND ACCESSORIES

The mouthpiece can make or mar an instrument, and as much trouble must be taken in the selection of this as of the instrument itself. Though it is advisable for it to be of the same make as the instrument this is not essential so long as the bore measurement is the same. If the latter is not so the instrument will play out of tune. The lay should be the standard English no. 2 or the equivalent, for this will give the tone quality wanted for classical music. It should be closely examined for flaws to the tip, along the rails or facing and inside the chamber. Ligatures vary and must be tested for a firm grip of the reed. A case should be chosen in which the instrument parts will stay securely in place and in which there is a compartment for reeds, grease and a swab. Finally, if the pupil does not have a music stand, now is the time to get him one, for without it he will develop a bad posture.

### CARE OF INSTRUMENT

Daily care of the clarinet consists first of swabbing out after blowing; this should be done with a pull-through and not a mop, for the latter tends to deposit fluff in the tone holes and its handle scratches the bore. Moisture should be dried from the joint recesses and from time to time the cork on the tenons lubricated with the special grease supplied or with ordinary Vaseline. If any pads have become soaked with moisture these should be dried out with cigarette papers; tissues or blotting paper are not suitable, for they leave particles behind. Persistent soaking of a pad means either that it is not seating properly or that the spring is not strong enough. Until a repair can be made the water can be diverted by an application of grease to the bore just above the offending hole. When the instrument is clean and dry it should be returned to its case to keep it free from dust.

A new wood clarinet loses a certain amount of its natural oil during the first few months of being blown. This should be replaced by applying special wood-dressing oil or olive oil. The oil should be painted on the outside of the instrument, moderately and taking care to avoid pads and keywork. The inside should be swabbed with a spare pull-through dipped in the oil. Manufacturers recommend the oiling to be done once a week for the first four weeks and then once a month for the following four months. The mechanism should be lubricated occasionally with a fine oil such as clock or sewing machine. Before this is done the instrument should be thoroughly dusted with a soft brush. Then, using a fine dipper, (a long handled pin is suitable), a small amount of oil is applied to each screw head, the working end of all needle springs, and the complete surface of flat springs. When the teacher does this job for the pupil he is provided with a good opportunity for seeing that the instrument is in good order, with no loose screws, bent keys or springs. He should also inspect the pupil's case from time to time to see that the instrument is being housed carefully.

The mouthpiece can harbour germs and should the pupil suffer any prolonged infection of the mouth or throat it is advisable to disinfect it either with the special fluid sold for all wind instruments or with a solution of warm water and dilute disinfectant of the household variety.

## REPAIRS

As no shop will loan a spare instrument while repairs are done the teacher should be able to do minor repairs for the pupil so that he does not have to be without. The pupil should watch these repairs so that he will be able one day to do them for himself. The materials the teacher will need are : a small screw-driver, a small pair of forceps, pipe cleaners, matches, razor knife, rags, methylated spirits, spare pads and screws, sheet cork in various thicknesses and shellac or water-proof glue. When pads have to be replaced the key should first be removed from the instrument. If the pad has been stuck in with shellac the latter can be softened by the application of heat (with match or bunsen burner) to the cup, but if a composition adhesive has been used the pad will have to be scraped out with a tool. Fresh shellac, previously softened with a little methylated spirits, is then applied to the cup and a new pad of the correct circumference and thickness inserted. If any of the cork has to be replaced it must be cut very exactly to measure and fixed in the same way as the pads.

A bent key is a common problem and it is again advisable to remove the key from the instrument before straightening, for the latter has to be done most carefully or the metal will fracture. If a ligature does not grip properly when fixed, a strip of thin cork or felt should be glued inside the band at the back. When the straight front edges of a ligature cut into the reed these must be rubbed down with a metal file.

## DETECTION OF FAULTS

If the pupil's clarinet produces notes in the clarinet register instead of the chalumeau then the fault can be traced to the break keys. The teacher should first check the adjustment of the screw on top of the g'♯ key. If this is correct, then the trouble will be either bad seating of one of the pads on the g'♯, a' or b'♭ keys, or a weak spring on one of these. If it is the former, the pad must be replaced. If the latter, then the spring will have to be adjusted or replaced and until this can be done a rubber band brought onto the instrument and fixed in such a way as to give pressure over the pad which is not closing properly will be effective. When no sound will come out of the instrument from a particular note downwards the cause is a leak in the pad immediately above this note. For a leak that is difficult to locate a smoke test should be carried out as follows : the bell of the clarinet is blocked with a pull-through and the instrument closed completely by placing all fingers on as if playing low e. Cigarette smoke is then blown into the instrument and will reveal the leak by emerging from the pad which is not sealing. Poor quality sound or fuzziness on a note which is produced by opening a key indicates either that the pad on this key is not venting sufficiently or that the surface of the pad is imperfect. Flatness *developing* on particular notes is caused by sediment collecting in the tone holes; this, most common in the break notes, can be corrected by cleaning the holes out with a pipe cleaner.

## GENERAL OVERHAUL

At some time during the final year of a would-be professional's training he should have a demonstration of how to do a general overhaul. This should be carried out on a suitable work-table (of non-slippery surface or covered with a cloth) placed in a good light. The teacher proceeds by stripping one joint, placing the screws and keys carefully in order as they are removed. The woodwork and keys are then thoroughly cleaned and any sediment removed from the holes with a pipe cleaner. Next, all necessary repairs to pads and corks are carried out and finally the silverwork polished. Each key is then replaced on the joint, in exactly the *reverse order* to that in which it was dismantled, the screws and springs all being given an application of oil in the process. An overhaul and check such as this should be carried out every few years. When an instrument is well looked after in this way a total re-pad is never necessary, and in fact is undesirable.

### SELECTION OF REEDS

On the subject of reeds Vanderhagen says : "A beginner is not best served by a strong reed because the lips are not used to gripping and this will make the instrument more difficult than necessary, and because strong reeds are liable to make the clarinet squeak and cause a quantity of air to escape from the sides of the mouth." A soft reed then is chosen for the pupil at his first lesson. As the pupil's muscles strengthen he will need more resistance, especially for producing the high notes, and should then go on to harder ones. Muscle quality only comes into the matter of choice in the initial stages; once the embouchure has acquired strength the lay of the mouthpiece is the governing factor. Thus if the mouthpiece has a standard no. 2 lay, reeds from the $1\frac{1}{2}$, 2 or $2\frac{1}{2}$ range should be used, the lower figure being for a narrow tip opening and the higher for a wide. Higher numbered mouthpiece lays require higher numbered reeds.

The teacher should keep a supply of good but moderately

priced reeds for the child pupil to select from. The pupil should be shown how to test first without the ligature, holding the reed to the mouthpiece with the hand and blowing g'. The teacher will guide him by describing the reed response as 'soft' or 'hard', explaining that these refer to ease or strength of blowing respectively and not to quality of sound. If the tone is good and the response easy the reed is then fixed with the ligature and tested again. At this stage it will have slightly more resistance because less of the reed is free to vibrate. If the resistance is too great a further selection must be made. It is not a good thing to try to 'blow in' a stiff reed, for in so doing the embouchure has to make an adaptation which is upsetting to the playing. Squeaking reeds should be thrown out for they will only cause tension in the player. Warped reeds will straighten if soaked overnight in cold water and then dried out flat side down on a sheet of glass.

When the pupil has to buy reeds at the shop he will not be able to blow them, so must be shown beforehand how to determine whether the spring or strength corresponds to those he is used to by gently flexing the tip with a finger. He should choose cane that is golden in colour, neither yellow nor green, and with straight and evenly-spaced grain, and should examine the kidney or thicker part of the blade against the light to see that it is well formed. Different makes of reed vary in their shaping, each one requiring an adaptation by the embouchure; in order not to upset the embouchure more than necessary it is therefore advisable to stick to one make, unless there is good reason to do otherwise.

### TREATMENT OF REEDS

In days gone by clarinet players had to make their own reeds and spent a great deal of time in the cutting and shaping of them. Today this is no longer necessary, thanks to the excellence of machine-made reeds. A reed which is immediately suitable for performance can be chosen, and as it softens with use the tip is kept at the right strength by clipping with a reed cutter. The reed will become too soggy or dirty before it is cut too short. It is important to keep the reed at the right strength or high notes become difficult and this puts a strain on the embouchure. Nothing but a purpose-built reed cutter should be used on the tip for this needs to be very clean cut. Until the pupil has one of his own he should be advised to change his reeds fairly frequently, setting the used ones aside to dry and stiffen up again. If he continues too long on one reed this makes it difficult for him to adapt to another. Some clarinettists advocate choosing a hard reed and scraping it down to suit. This process takes considerable time and is by no means always satisfactory, so that it would seem to create a 'reed problem' where none need exist.

As reeds are fragile and expensive the pupil must be encouraged to cap his reed, taking particular care not to chip it, as soon as he has finished playing. In swabbing out the clarinet the reed has to be removed, but should be put back on the mouthpiece afterwards so that it retains its shape and will blow the same next time. Pupils should be warned from rubbing a dirty finger or thumb along the shaped surface of the reed, for dirt here can set up inflammation of the lip, if the latter is at all cracked. Reeds harbour germs too and if at any time a pupil has a bad mouth infection the reed he last used should be destroyed.

# 4

# *Preliminaries: Basic Method*

## ASSEMBLING THE INSTRUMENT

Learning how to assemble and dismantle the clarinet, though a necessary part of the first lesson, is of minor interest to the beginner compared with the actual blowing of the instrument, and so this procedure should be delayed until that stage when the pupil begins to find the weight of the instrument on his thumb too much for him and needs a rest from holding it. The teacher therefore puts the clarinet together himself without comment at the beginning of the lesson and proceeds with the much-looked-forward-to instruction on playing. When a pause becomes necessary the pupil will learn first how to *dismantle* the instrument, in the following way: his attention is drawn to the correct positioning of the two link keys at the centre joint then, holding the bottom joint with his left hand and placing the ball of his right hand on the rings of the top joint to raise the top link key, he is shown how to twist the top joint off, taking the side keys in the direction of the thumb-rest. He can then remove the mouthpiece, barrel and bell without special instruction, for there are no problems here. The whole process is then practised in the reverse order for re-assembly.

## FIXING THE REED

Then should follow some information on his reed. The pupil

is told that it responds more easily when wet and is instructed to moisten it thoroughly on the flat side. If the tip warps in the process it should be held firmly with the thumb against the table of the mouthpiece for a minute and this will flatten it. The pupil should then hold his mouthpiece at eye level and place his reed against it, just below the tip. In so doing he must hold the base of the reed with one hand and manoeuvre it from the sides with the other, avoiding touching the tip with his fingers. The ligature is then brought down over the reed to below the mouthpiece opening, being careful not to damage the tip of the reed in the process. Some mouthpieces have guide lines to show the position of the ligature, but these are not always accurate. The important point is that the reed should not be clamped over the *opening* of the mouthpiece, for this part must be completely free to vibrate. The ligature is specially shaped to take the reed under its screws and these must be centralized at the front of the mouthpiece. It should not be turned with the screws at the back, for the rounded side will then cut across the sides of the reed. The screws should be just tight enough to grip; if too tight they may cause the mouthpiece to warp.

### PARENT CO-OPERATION

The assembling of the instrument and fixing of the reed are difficult enough for an adult beginner. For a young child they are extraordinarily difficult and the teacher is strongly advised to ask for a parent to be present at the first lesson so that assistance can be given with this matter at home. The parent should also be co-opted into being with the child when he practises, for he needs all the help and encouragement he can get in the initial stages.

## OVERALL PLAN

The basic method which is set out in the following pages can be applied to every type of beginner and embraces the general manipulation of the instrument as well as the correct sequence of notes. The sequence of notes is extremely important and should be followed scrupulously, even if this means a deviation from the chosen tutor. The speed with which the notes are introduced will vary according to the age and ability of the pupil and although the method is set out for a young child beginner who cannot manage more than two notes at the first lesson, the older beginner or the one who has had previous musical experience may well manage to advance in the same time into the 'next steps' section. The teacher should have his own instrument out and give demonstrations at each step, then ensure that the step is mastered by the pupil before going on to the next. All symbols should be written down for the pupil as they are introduced. Fingering diagrams should be drawn with the bell at the top of the picture so that the pupil finds what he wants by looking down the instrument, keeping it in the playing position. (For example, see chapter 6.) The old method with the diagram the other way up is not satisfactory for it means the pupil has to visualize the fingering as if in a mirror, or else take his instrument out of the playing position to study it from the front. This method leads to all sorts of uncertainties in fingering, especially with regard to the little fingers.

## PLAYING POSITION

Whatever his age it is advisable for the pupil to sit to begin with for this avoids unnecessary fatigue. He should sit away from the back of the chair and slightly forward, so that the breath does not have to come 'up hill'. The elbows should be away from the sides and the feet uncrossed, again so that the breathing is not interfered with.

### FIRST SOUND

In order that the pupil can give his whole mind to the embouchure when producing his first sound, only the mouthpiece and barrel joint are used. The teacher, using his own components, asks the pupil to watch closely while he forms an embouchure and demonstrates a note. The pupil is then told to stretch his bottom lip over the teeth, and the teacher guides him to place the mouthpiece, reed downwards and with slight pressure, on to the lip. The pupil then rests his top teeth on the mouthpiece and lets the top lip fall to enclose it. He is next to point his tongue and place it, just back from its tip, gently against the reed tip. As he blows the note he is to withdraw his tongue smartly, articulating the syllable *tee*. After several sounds have been satisfactorily produced in this manner the reed is capped for safety and both barrel and mouthpiece put back on to the clarinet for the next step.

### HOLDING THE INSTRUMENT

The note which is easiest for the pupil to start on is e′, requiring the use of only the left thumb and index finger. However, if he is allowed to play this straight away, without instruction first on the placing of all digits and proper balance of the instrument, the result will be a bunching up of the fingers of both hands and an insecure balance which will be difficult to put right later on. So, resting the bell of the clarinet on a knee and holding on to the barrel with the left hand, the pupil is first taught to place the index, middle and ring fingers of the right hand correctly. He must cover the rings as well as the holes and with the pads of his fingers, not the tips. The right thumb is then put under the thumb-rest, just over the first joint towards the tip. Now the clarinet can be lifted from the knee and held in a central position with the right hand. The left hand is removed from the barrel and its index, middle and ring fingers placed in the same way as for the right. The left thumb is then placed on both hole and speaker key. At this stage it is as well to check the holding angle of the instrument. This is given by Thomas Lindsay Willman in *A Complete Instruction Book for the Clarinet* (London 1826) where he says: "A Plumb line falling from between the Collar Bone, gives the distance of the Bell of the Clarinet, which is Nine Inches & a half from the Body." Finally, making sure the middle fingers of both hands are at right angles to the instrument, the right little finger is placed on the f key and the left on the e. The pupil should then be given a minute or two to hold this position and become accustomed to it. At the same time the teacher should check that he is keeping his shoulders square, for the position of the right hand below the left and the weight of the instrument tend to pull the body down on the right. Whilst all this takes a long time to write, it takes next to no time to conduct the pupil through it and will not delay him unduly. It should be done and is capital invested, for it will pay dividends later.

## CONTINUATION OF FIRST LESSON

The pupil now prepares to play e'. The little fingers are to remain on their keys during the learning of all the left hand notes, for this will greatly assist in keeping both hands permanently in a good position. The pupil is told to *tip* (not slide) the left thumb off the speaker key and, keeping this thumb and left index finger in place, to lift all others a mere half inch off their holes. *Bringing the clarinet up to his mouth* (not taking his head down to the clarinet) the pupil will then attempt the note. If the sound does not at first come the pupil is probably pressing too hard against the reed and closing the aperture between it and the mouthpiece. Putting more mouthpiece in will overcome this difficulty. If the air goes through the reed but does not produce a note, then less mouthpiece is the answer. Experimentation at this stage is important until the happy mean is found. (See also Chapter 6 for correct mouthpiece position.) When the note comes easily the pupil should sustain it on as long a breath as he can manage. If his tone is pinched then he is probably tightening his throat and must be told to relax it.

The semibreve is the first symbol to be introduced, and one is then played on e', tapping the beats out with the foot. The note should be stopped *at the end* of the fourth beat by the tongue returning lightly to the reed, e.g. : 1 2 3 4 stop. Next, a series of semibreves is introduced, starting each one with a tongue stroke, but not stopping on the reed until the end of the final note. One note alone is not music and so if possible at the first lesson d' should be introduced as well. Before the note is blown the teacher should check that the pupil's little fingers are still on their keys, and give him some practice in placing the middle finger of the left hand well and truly over both ring and hole.

### SECOND LESSON—THUMB TROUBLES

It quite often happens that the pupil arrives for his second lesson in a state of despair that his right thumb is unbearably painful, because of the weight of the instrument. This is a condition which must be put right straight away for otherwise it is enough to discourage the pupil to the point of stopping. The weight can be removed from the hand by lodging the bell of the instrument on a music stand screw which has been adjusted to a suitable height. (N.B. The stand should always be set up with a single leg centralized at the back, so that any pressure against it is supported.) This remedy is more suitable than allowing the pupil to rest the clarinet on a knee, because this causes a tension to one side. It should however only be allowed in moderation, for otherwise the pupil tends not to use his right thumb and removes it from the thumb-rest. Another source of trouble is a hard thumb-rest; this can be made more comfortable by cushioning with foam rubber.

### FAULTS

One of the commonest faults at the very beginning is blowing the cheeks out. If the pupil can be taught to dimple the cheeks this will bring them in by dispelling the pocket of air between them and the teeth. If he cannot do this he should try holding his cheeks in with his left hand whilst blowing open g'. The teacher may need to assist the latter operation by holding the clarinet steady. Another early fault is the clarinet wobbling in the lips; this means the top lip is being used too much, causing the top teeth to float instead of resting on the mouthpiece. A special watch will be needed on those pupils who have previously played the recorder, for the following faults are likely to occur : insufficient force of breath being used, too much mouthpiece put in and the top teeth not resting on it, tonguing from the roof of the mouth or back of the top teeth, tips of fingers instead of pads being used, fingers covering holes only and not the rings (the left thumb especially needs watching because of half-holing on the recorder), and fingers not in use trying to support the instrument.

NEXT STEPS

The second lesson should introduce f'♯, the slur sign and breath marks. When slurring the pupil will need help in resisting the impulse to tongue with each foot tap or change of note. Next lesson will bring c', g' and the semibreve rest symbol. The pupil's appreciation of a rest is greatly enhanced if it is suggested he returns his tongue lightly to the reed for its duration. Although this is not normal procedure on a rest after a sustained note, it is so after a staccato note and will stand him in good stead for this. The lesson immediately following will introduce the true staccato, where it is imperative for the tongue to return quickly to the reed after the note has been sounded (see Chapter 7). The next notes to be learnt are b, a and g. For these the little fingers should be taken off their keys but kept close above them. Now can follow basic instruction on scales, for all the notes in the scale of G major have been learnt. The scale of G should then be practised, downwards first. On coming up, the pupil may start lifting his fingers too high; the teacher can prevent this by holding his hand over them at a suitable height. The arpeggio of G is next introduced and this affords useful practice in the synchronization of fingers moved in combination. The next notes to be learnt are f'♮, b♭ and f. In playing the latter the pupil must turn his right wrist away from the side keys to bring the little finger over its key and enable the ring finger to close its hole properly. Now follow the scale and arpeggio of F major. The scale is the easiest on the clarinet and presents no problems; in the arpeggio some practice will be needed in lifting the right ring and little fingers together and placing them back carefully, also in keeping the clarinet steady when moving from c′ to f′. After this bottom e is learnt and here, as in the case of f, the wrist must be turned towards the little finger to enable the ring finger to cover its hole well. 'Break a″' is learnt by first playing f′♯ and then tipping over on to the side of the finger for the a′ key. The wrist must be kept flexible for tipping and the finger should not be allowed to slide up the a′ key but must stay on the tip of it. 'Break b′♭' is then learnt by a similar method, the note being approached from the f′♮ and the wrist being turned in the opposite direction to the previous manoeuvre, in opening the thumb key. As in the pupil's first instruction on holding the instrument, the thumb must close its hole with only one side of its pad, the other side being used to open the speaker key.

## CROSSING THE FIRST BREAK

Now comes 'crossing the break', often considered to be the 'bugbear' of clarinet playing, but which is in truth not so very difficult if the above-mentioned position of left thumb plus wrist movement has been mastered. If the latter has not been mastered and the thumb is allowed to slide up to the speaker key, a break in the sound will occur every time the register is changed. A tendency also develops to lower the clarinet and raise the angle of the head when changing to the higher register. Because the clarinet overblows at a twelfth and not an octave the pupil now has to adjust to the fact that fingerings in the clarinet register produce notes with a different letter-name than in the chalumeau register. To help him to adjust the teacher should write out all exercises at this stage with the letters under the notes. As a preliminary to crossing the break, the afore-mentioned thumb position and wrist movement should be practised in the 'jumping 12ths' exercise which follows :

The little finger notes are involved in crossing the break and as these are more difficult to get in the clarinet register, some practice on them should follow next :

Crossing the break itself should in the first instance be approached in a downward direction because it is easier to lift several fingers at once than to put them down together. In the following exercises all the right hand and the left little finger can remain down for a', because this does not affect the pitch of the note and will greatly facilitate coming up again. It is important for the pupil to use a good left wrist movement when going to and from the a' key, and to keep his blowing continuous.

### ATTENDANT DIFFICULTIES

Those with slim fingers suffer most at the stage just reached. They will always have found it difficult to cover holes adequately and now the use of the speaker key increases their difficulty, especially with regard to the left ring finger. If the pupil has really exceptional trouble getting over this difficulty the teacher should advise him, if he can afford the extra cost, to exchange his instrument for a 'covered Boehm'. This instrument is similar in construction to the flute in which all holes are pad-covered, and will entirely solve the problem. The child pupil with a small hand and the elderly pupil with an arthritic hand may complain at this stage of more pain in the right thumb. This can be alleviated by fixing to their instrument a sling similar to that used by a saxophonist or bassoonist. It will be necessary to have a small ring soldered on to the top of the thumb rest by the instrument shop, who will also supply the sling. The latter is threaded through the ring, looped round the back of the neck and adjusted so that the weight of the instrument is taken away from the thumb.

### NEW REGISTER

The scales and arpeggios of G and F are now learnt in a two octave range, downwards first because it is physically easier, and then upwards. In the ascending scale of G during the progression from b′ to c″ some unnecessary mechanical movement can be eliminated and a smoother progression ensured by putting both keys down together for b′. To familiarize the pupil with the nomenclature of the new register some of his early pieces can be used again, transposed up a twelfth. It will be seen that in this way the fingering remains the same while the note letters are changed.

Bb major scale and arpeggio are the next to be learnt. These involve the use of two new keys, the first side key and the e″b (ab) key. The right wrist must be flexible in going to the side key and at the same time the fingers must adjust so that they remain curved over their holes. The following exercise will afford practice of the movement and accustom the pupil to using it in context :

This exercise can be used again an octave higher to give practice in using the e″♭ key. In coming down to this key from above, the difficulty is to cover the lowest hole adequately with the ring finger. If, as in the recommended exercise, a good finger position is established first by starting below the e″♭, the difficulty is more easily overcome.

The learning of scales is made considerably more difficult for the clarinettist because of the instrument overblowing at a twelfth. It is therefore important to give him a good practice formula. He should first be drilled, as any instrumentalist should, in saying backwards the seven letters used in music, otherwise he will always have difficulty coming down the scale. The following formula can then be put into practice :

1. Say the letter sequence of the scale, going both up and down.
2. Say the letters whilst fingering the notes, up and down.
3. Play the scale, going up and down.

### CROSSING THE SECOND BREAK

The pupil is now ready for the final stage, that of crossing the top break. In the same way that notes a twelfth above the chalumeau register became possible by opening the speaker key, so notes a sixth above the clarinet register can be obtained by opening the top finger hole. What actually happens is that by opening the speaker key the clarinet's third harmonic is obtained and by opening the top hole its fifth harmonic is encouraged. The fifth harmonic does not come easily if the left index finger lifts sharply upwards from its hole, but it does if the hole is opened gradually by the finger being removed sideways towards the middle finger. The teacher should give the following exercise to accustom the pupil to this movement, and as with the other change of register it is advisable to write the letters in. The best fingering for top d'''♯ is the forked; therefore both notes in the third bar should have this fingering. In every bar, after sliding the index finger off it should be repositioned over its hole again.

E C♯  F D  F♯ D♯  G E

D major scale and arpeggio should now be learnt. In descending the scale, during the progression from c''♯ to b', unnecessary mechanical movement can again be avoided by putting both keys down for c''♯. This makes a smoother progression and eliminates noisy key clatter.

### ADJUSTMENT OF EMBOUCHURE

Each new register requires a slight adjustment of embouchure and the higher the notes are the more lip pressure is needed against the reed. This must be explained to the pupil, otherwise in his efforts to produce the notes he will simply blow much harder and not use his lips properly. A harder reed will be a help to him at this stage. If the pupil has extreme difficulty in getting high notes then a very hard reed (which should only be used as a temporary measure), will produce the pitch for him and give a feel of what is required from the lip.

Having learnt tightness of embouchure for high notes the pupil has then to be reminded to slacken as he comes down in pitch otherwise squeaks (which are in reality harmonics), will occur on lower notes, especially those on the break.

### SUMMARY

All steps calling for a particular method or order of learning have now been dealt with. The teacher will introduce remaining notes and keys, new rhythmic patterns, expression marks, etc., as and when he thinks fit. He will find guidance in the ensuing chapters on all the principal features of playing the clarinet; each is considered individually and in detail. One final point needs to be emphasized before leaving this chapter: the teacher should watch every time the pupil begins to play that the preliminaries to blowing are correctly and unhurriedly made, so that his first note is always of the best. These preliminaries are: fingers on, clarinet in, breathe in, close embouchure, tongue on reed and *pause* to consider the note to be made.

# 5
## *Breathing*

Frédéric Berr writes in his *Traité complet de Clarinette* (Paris 1836) that "the air column should always remain at the disposal of the executant". Control of the air column requires a knowledge of the physical processes employed in breathing and whilst the pupil does not require an elaborate explanation of this the teacher needs to be perfectly clear on what is involved. The question of *how* to breath will be dealt with in the present chapter, that of *when* to breathe is considered in Chapter 10, for this is closely bound up with interpretation.

### PHYSICAL PROCESS DESCRIBED

The generator of energy for breathing is the diaphragm, and its proper use with the full expansion of the lungs is the secret of good control. The diaphragm is a large muscular membrane which separates the chest from the abdomen. The lungs are sponge-like sacks enclosed within the ribs and occupying the whole region of the chest except for the small compartment containing the heart. At rest the diaphragm is arched into the chest, but when inhalation takes place it contracts, pulling the floor of the chest downwards and forwards. Simultaneously the lower ribs expand, causing the lungs to draw in air through the windpipe. At the top of the windpipe is the glottis, which closes when required, acting as a stopper to this human compression chamber. In exhalation the contracted diaphragm yields to pressure from the abdominal muscles and the air in the lungs is pushed out again through the windpipe. The speed with which this is done must be governed in order to play a sustained phrase. To maintain the compression element the rib cage is kept raised and only on the final emptying of the lungs does it fall.

### INHALATION

Whether standing or sitting the pupil should adopt a natural upright position with backbone extended. If he is sitting he should not lean against the back of the chair or cross his legs, both of which interfere with the correct breathing process. Before breath is taken in, the clarinet should be raised to the playing position with elbows away from the sides to assist full expansion of the ribs. It is immaterial whether first breaths are taken through the nose or mouth, but during the course of the music it is quicker and quieter to take breath in through the corners of the mouth. In either case, the shoulders must not be raised or this will cause muscular tension in arms, hands and fingers. Neither must the throat be allowed to tighten in the process, but should be kept well open throughout both inhalation and exhalation. The pupil should be encouraged to feel his rib expansion, not only in the front but at the sides and the back. Rib expansion is responsible for two-thirds of the air-gain in fully inflated lungs, the other third being due to the descent of the diaphragm. The lungs attain their largest capacity in the back and lowest sections, and it is quite wrong to try to produce a big bulge below the breast bone, for this is too high and will not allow correct action of the abdominal muscles. It is equally wrong to try to distend the lower abdomen in order to make the diaphragm descend further. Such distension is usually accompanied by relaxation of the ribs and consequent loss of breath control. It also causes undue pressure on the abdominal organs and for this reason alone must be corrected.

## EXHALATION

In exhaling, the pupil should project the sound right through the bell end of the clarinet to beyond, for unless this is done the tone is thin and breathy. Berr maintains that the best sound is produced if the air is emitted along an elevated line which passes under the fingers, using them as the roof of the tube. The softer the sound the more energy is required to control the expiratory process. Any pulling in or tightening of the waist during exhalation is wrong, but the waist does of its own accord become smaller when the diaphragm relaxes. To retain control of the breathing process in prolonged playing the ribs should be held up to support a reserve of air, and for this reason the teacher should see that the pupil keeps in a good upright position. If breathing is properly controlled and enough breaths taken according to the musical content it should not be necessary to collapse the ribs and deflate the lungs completely until there is a suitable rest period. When a rest period does occur it should be taken advantage of to get rid of the last drop of stale air, which is harmful if kept too long in the lungs.

## PLANNING

When uninterrupted playing is prolonged, a build-up of pressure can occur which is distressing. To combat this, until the lungs have a chance to empty and recover, half instead of full breaths can be taken, provided the phrases are short. Wind music should be played at the correct speed as soon as technique will allow, because of the strain on breathing otherwise. Until technique does allow, extra breaths must be carefully planned. The importance of planning breathing cannot be over-estimated (see Chapter 10), for if breath begins to run short this causes first panic which leads to stumbling over notes and then to collapse of the party !

## PRACTISING

From the commencement of his studies the pupil should be made to practise long notes to develop his power of sustaining the sound. A stimulus to length can be given by tapping the foot or timing with a second hand. Children should manage 20 seconds, adults 25 to 45 seconds. Care should be taken that the pupil does not let the rib cage fall as soon as the note starts. If he complains of an aching chest from keeping the ribs up this means he has not habitually filled his lungs. Reassure him, for the ache will subside and is not injurious. Long sustained notes and phrases are not the only breathing exercises; the art of snatching a quick breath should also be learnt at an early stage. A sustained tone is used for practising this, interrupting it every few counts to snatch breath and proceeding immediately after in the same manner as before. Quick intake of air is made through the corners of the mouth, without tensing the throat muscles and in such a way that the lip pressure against the reed is not disturbed, nor the upper lip dislodged from the top of the mouthpiece. These precautions must be taken or embouchure control will be lost for the succeeding note.

# 6

# Embouchure, Tone and Intonation

The word embouchure applied to a wind instrument denotes the position and control of the jaws, lips and surrounding muscles in tone production. Given a good embouchure, good quality tone and good intonation will result. These are balancing factors and the successful production of one will give the other. Their combination supplies what may be called 'the centre of the note'. The late Frederick Thurston, whose tone was superlatively beautiful, considered that to get a good quality tone the pupil needed to come with it already in his 'mind's ear'. The pupil who has been inspired to learn by hearing a good player usually does this, but if the pupil does not have a criterion then his teacher must give him one.

## EMBOUCHURE POSITION

To control sound on the clarinet pressure in varying degrees is applied to the reed by the lower jaw through the lip at the point *where the reed becomes one with the mouthpiece*; that is to say, at the end of the mouthpiece lay. From this it will be seen that the position of the embouchure on the mouthpiece is determined by the length of mouthpiece lay. The teacher must examine the pupil's mouthpiece and determine the length of lay, then indicate its termination by drawing a pencil line across the reed for the pupil's guidance. The pupil then places his lower jaw according to this line, rests his top teeth on the mouthpiece and closes the lips around to prevent escape of air. (See Chapter 4.) If too much reed is put in there will be excessive effort in blowing and probably escape of air, whereas not enough reed will give a thin, restricted tone. The exact amount must be found, the feel of it established and the embouchure developed in this position. Once substantially formed the embouchure will not let the player down and although he may be conscious of slight deviations in his tone when using different reeds his listeners will not.

### LONG NOTES

John Mahon, in *The New and Complete Preceptor for the Clarinet* (London 1803) insists that long notes should be practised to "acquire a firmness of the Lips, or Embouchure, and proper government of the Reed, which is the foundation of good Tone." The same holds good today and the teacher should make a rule of long notes at the beginning of every lesson and every practice. The notes should be started without the tongue, so that the lips are in control throughout. They should be played with a crescendo on the first half breath and a decrescendo on the second, and during these changes of dynamic care should be taken that tone quality does not alter. Dynamic variations are made by variations of breath pressure and the tendency will be for the tone to become harsh when the blowing is hard and breathy when it is gentle. These undesirable qualities are due to a slackening of the sideways tension of the lips. Provided this tension is kept up there is no reason why the clarinet's full range of dynamics should not be used.

### CONSISTENCY OF LIP PRESSURE
### IN DYNAMIC VARIATION

Dynamic variations must not be allowed to affect lip pressure, otherwise the pitch will alter. The inexperienced player loosens his embouchure as he blows harder in the crescendo and this causes the pitch to drop; he then tightens as he blows softer and the pitch rises. He must learn to keep his lip pressure constant throughout changes of dynamic. The following exercises are designed to make him fully conscious of the responsibility of his lips by giving him extremes of dynamic to cope with. In each exercise he should tongue the beginning of the sustained note, taking care in so doing that he does not upset his embouchure. The changes of dynamic should be immediate.

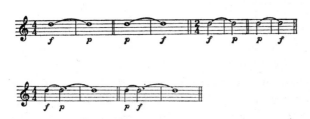

### ADAPTATION OF EMBOUCHURE
### IN PITCH VARIATION

The embouchure does alter when pitch alters, adopting a slacker hold for lower notes and a tighter one for higher. This alteration is necessary not only to obtain the correct pitch but also to maintain good quality tone. Pupils with a good ear make the alteration naturally, but others must be shown how to do it. There are two features involved in the alteration : flexibility of jaw and a changing mouth cavity. Thus, in going through the full range of notes from lowest to highest, the lower jaw is gradually raised and the mouth alters shape as if for the following vowels: *aw-ah-eh-ee*. The pupil should first practise this alteration on scales from bottom to top and back again.

During the manœuvre it is important that the bottom lip remains stretched against the reed otherwise tone quality is lost. After this the pupil is given wide intervals to pitch. Here the mouth changes are more marked and he must be taught to anticipate his embouchure *before* changing to the next note. Octaves are the easiest interval for the pupil to know whether he is playing in tune and therefore making the alteration of embouchure correctly, so he should practise these slurred and tongued, both upwards and downwards.

## HIGH NOTES AND THE EMBOUCHURE

The embouchure requires quite considerable muscle strength for the highest notes. To develop this the pupil should play long notes in this register, starting them loudly with the tongue and continuing on a decrescendo. This should be followed by exercises slurring up to the register from an octave below. Giving extra lip pressure for high notes sometimes causes the mouth to creep back on the reed, transferring the point of control to the wrong place. This may have the unfortunate result of closing the reed up. To counteract this the right thumb should be pushed slightly up while playing and this will keep the lip pressure well down on to the thicker part of the reed, where it should be. In persistent difficulty with the high notes the pupil should try going farther down the reed than his norm. This will force the necessary harmonic through and when he has had experience of it in this way he will be able to produce it from the correct embouchure position. The notes d‴ and e‴ can be more troublesome to produce properly than those higher up. This is due not so much to lack of muscle power but to insecurity of embouchure. To encourage faith in his embouchure the pupil should be given plenty of long notes on f‴ and f‴♯, fingering them the 'long' way, thus:

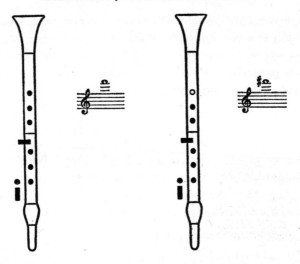

The 'long' fingering makes these notes easier to produce than when the fingering with less holes covered is used. In the same way, if the pupil has difficulty with g''' and a''', then some practice on top b'''♭ fingered as follows will help:

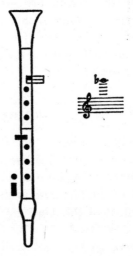

High notes are considerably easier to play on the A clarinet, the pitch of a semitone lower making a surprising difference in this respect. If therefore the pupil has an A this should be used in preference to his B♭ for his first altissimo practice and this will lessen the strain on his embouchure.

### EMBOUCHURE CHECKING

High note practice can be unsettling to the embouchure and it is important for the teacher to check the pupil's position on the reed from time to time. If playing is allowed in the wrong position the following faults are likely to occur :

1. Harmonics or 'squeaks' on lower notes, due to too much reed in and too much lip pressure.
2. An undertone on higher notes because the necessary harmonic is not able to come through, due to too little reed in with not enough lip pressure.

If in doubt about the line of pressure on the reed some experimentation should be made with the notes g″♯, a″ and b″♭. These notes are peculiarly sensitive and if the exact embouchure position can be found for them, it will be correct for the rest of the instrument.

### TONE QUALITY AND TUNING PECULIARITIES

The tone quality of the clarinet is not consistent throughout its range, but the weak notes can be improved a certain amount by practising slurring from a 'good' note to a 'bad', carrying the quality of the first over to the second. The notes most needing treatment of this kind are those on the break, and also g♯/d″♯, c′♯/g″♯ and d′♯/a″♯. Tuning is also inconsistent on the clarinet. In its 'cold' position with the barrel joint pushed in, the notes at the bell end tend to be flat, whilst the break and throat notes tend to be sharp. As the clarinet warms the pitch rises and the barrel joint must be pulled out to compensate for this. There comes a point in this operation where the overall tuning becomes correct. However, if a further rise in pitch necessitates pulling the barrel out further then, whilst the end of the instrument may remain satisfactory, the break and throat notes become flat. All these irregularities of pitch affecting individual notes have to be compensated for by the lips which should tighten to raise the pitch and slacken to lower it (see following section). The pupil must have regular practice in playing under all three tuning conditions —barrel joint in, pulled out a little, and pulled out more— and get used to the embouchure adjustments that have to be made. Even when not playing with another instrument his clarinet must be kept tuned to the right pitch, both in his lesson and his practice, and this in time will make his responses to pitch automatic.

## TUNING BY LIPS—VIBRATO

When tightening and slackening of the embouchure takes place on one note, causing a fluctuation of pitch, this is known as vibrato. It follows then that if the pupil practises vibrato he will acquire ability to keep his tuning correct. The area most amenable to pitch alteration is the top end of the instrument. So, choosing one of the throat or break notes, the teacher makes the pupil first blow the note normally, with a mouth shape equivalent to *ah*. Then he is to slacken his jaw to produce a mouth shape of *aw* and a lowering of pitch, and from there proceed through the vowels *ah* and *eh* to *ee*, sharpening as he goes, and then back again in one continuous movement. The object of the manœuvre is to obtain as much variation of

E

pitch as possible. The jaw must not drop too much in the *aw* shape or the lip will lose control of the reed. Its movement should be slow when the exercise is first practised and when pitch variation has been established its speed can be increased. After practising in the throat and break note areas the pupil should perform the exercise throughout the range of the instrument. There are players who use vibrato and the tremolo indiscriminately for effect during the course of their performance. Far from heightening the intensity this tends to deprive the delivery of conviction and is not recommended. Instead, if the tone is kept firm and steady and emotional intensity created through carefully studied dynamics the player is much more likely to capture the heart of the audience.

## TUNING BY FINGERING

The embouchure can be assisted in the tuning of particular areas by the following fingering devices :

1. Sharp break notes can be lowered in pitch by placing the middle and ring fingers of the left hand on their holes.

2. Flat notes above b″ can be brought up to pitch by placing the right little finger on the g♯/d″♯ key. This should *not* be done however for d‴♯ and e‴ because the seventh harmonic then becomes too strong, resulting in the pitching of g‴♯ and a‴ instead.

3. Flat very high notes can be brought up to pitch considerably by using either one of the ring finger keys.

## INCORRECT PITCH

General overall flatness in a beginner pupil should rectify itself as his embouchure improves and is strengthened by use, but he must be made aware of the flatness and encouraged to tighten his lips as much as he can. If after some time he is still unable to play up to pitch then the barrel joint must be shortened to make the instrument itself play sharper. If a pupil who has formerly played in tune *develops* flatness this usually means his reed has become too soft. Conversely, an overall sharpness can be caused by too hard a reed. If, after trying a softer reed and slackening the embouchure pitch is still too high, then a longer barrel should be advised. The pupil must then adapt his embouchure to lengthened-tube tuning. It is sometimes found after a pupil has been on his own for a long time that he is playing everything flat. This only means a lazy lip; if he has a session of playing with the piano again his ear will soon make him correct the lip tension.

### INTONATION PROBLEMS

Finally, it is necessary to mention occasions on which particular attention should be given to intonation. These are :

1. An initial entry.
2. The resumption of a phrase after a snatched breath.
3. The end of a long spell of continuous playing.

In the case of an initial entry the pupil must be trained to form an embouchure of the correct tension for the pitch of the note *before playing it*. In snatching a breath during a phrase the tendency is to relax the lips and then play the next note flat. The lip pressure must at all costs be kept up and the pupil should practise this during the course of a long note which is broken at intervals by breaths snatched through the corners of the mouth. During a long spell of continuous playing the pupil tends to go out of tune through exhaustion and the direction this takes will vary according to whether he is a beginner or

one of some experience. The beginner will go flat because his
lip muscles are not strong enough to keep up the tension. It
is a mistake to let him go on under these conditions for his
tone will become breathy and even non-existent under the
strain. He must be given a short rest before trying again. The
pupil of experience will go sharp because exhaustion has
caused undue lip tension. This will be more noticeable if the
music is soft and in the lower register. The problem will be
overcome by finding an appropriate point in the music at
which a conscious loosening of the embouchure can be made
and kept to the end.

# 7
# *Tonguing*

Lefèvre, in his *Méthode de Clarinette* (Paris 1802) states: "Articulation by stringed instruments is produced either through the medium of a bow, as for example on the violin, or with the fingers, as on the harp or guitar; that by wind instruments is made with the tongue. Without the tongue it is impossible to play the clarinet well, for it is to this instrument what the bow is to the violin."

Likewise the clarinettist who does not use his tongue properly can be compared to the singer who articulates unsatisfactorily and conveys no meaning with his words. The tongue's primary business is to start the sound by releasing the reed at a given moment and thus allowing it to vibrate in response to the breath pressure. It has a secondary business, to halt the sound by returning to the reed and stopping the vibrations, when the note is required to stop abruptly, such as in staccato. The sound is otherwise stopped by allowing the breath to cease. Because articulation is so much a part of tone production it is important that the pupil learns it with his first sound (see Chapter 4). There are however some teachers who take the view that it is too much for the pupil to have to do it at the beginning. This is a mistake, for the pupil then gets used to playing without articulation and when asked to add it finds that his tongue gets in the way and is most reluctant to do it.

## BASIC PROCEDURE

In preparing the first tongue movement the teacher asks the pupil to point his tongue and place it at the back of the reed tip. He should avoid saying "on the tip of the reed" for the pupil is then likely to go over the tip, touching this on the underside of the tongue. The point of contact is just below the reed tip and about an eighth to quarter inch back on the upper side of the tongue. The pupil begins the sound by pronouncing the word *tee* as he withdraws his tongue and releases his breath at the same time. The consonant *t* is chosen in preference to *d* for this brings a smaller area of tongue into contact with the reed and ensures a more nimble removal. The vowel *ee* is chosen because this is helpful to the beginner in the formation of his embouchure. It ensures a fairly close jaw position which will keep the lips stretched and the cheeks held in and the note up to pitch. If one of the more rounded vowels is used the common fault of dropping the jaw with the tongue movement is likely to occur and the note will be flat. When the embouchure has become firmer then the vowel sound appropriate to the register will be used, otherwise both tone quality and pitch will be wrong.

## FAULTS

Bubbles in the reed are a common source of annoyance at the beginning, but with experience the tip of the tongue can be kept free of excessive moisture so that they do not occur. They should be cleared by a sharp intake of breath through the reed and not by pressing or rubbing it; the latter method is ineffective and damaging to the reed. If the problem persists it probably means the flat surface of the reed has become greasy, causing the moisture to collect instead of flowing freely down into the clarinet. In this case the reed should be removed, rinsed in a mild detergent solution and left to dry out flat side down on a sheet of glass. It may be advisable to treat the mouthpiece rails also with detergent.

Most teachers experience the self-taught or badly-taught pupil who comes to them producing an accent on every tongued note. The cause of this phenomenon is the tongue pressing hard against the reed, the breath then having to be forced through at too great a speed, producing a loud sound. The pupil does not know that the tongue's sole purpose is to allow the reed to start vibrating, that the tongue does not require to give the reed a push. If his tongue pressure is relaxed then the reed is free to vibrate with whatever speed of air is required. Another fault which is found in new pupils who are not beginners is that of tonguing by remote control. This they do in one of three ways :

1. Starting the initial movement from inside the mouth, necessitating a double action of to and from the reed.
2. Starting all movements from the roof of the mouth and not touching the reed at all.
3. (Rarer) Ditto, from the lower lip.

In each case a delay and uncertainty of attack will be present. The sooner the pupil is converted to the correct method of articulation the better.

## SPEED

Speed in tonguing depends on the rate with which the tongue returns to the reed for each successive stroke, and to acquire a high speed the removal distance from the reed must be minimal. The control needed for this can only be attained by building up the tongue's strength in much regular practice. When strength and control have been acquired, the clarinettist should be able to single-tongue as fast as any music requires, rendering attempts at double- and triple-tonguing, which are not satisfactory on the instrument, unnecessary.

### DEVELOPING STRENGTH

The pupil's first exercise to develop tongue strength is to repeat a single short note in the low register followed by rests: e.g. ♪. The tongue is removed from the reed a short distance only and returned to it for the rests, quickly but lightly. It *remains on the reed* until it is time to remove it for the next note. This exercise is then modified by a shorter space of rest, and finally by elimination of rests altogether. In its latter form the note repetitions should be as fast as the pupil can manage and kept absolutely rhythmical. To encourage uniformity of tongue strokes no accents should be made in the early stages. Later, accents should be introduced, the teacher taking care that these are produced in the correct manner by stronger blowing. Accents must in no way affect the tongue stroke. Tone quality must be as good in staccato as legato playing and if it is found to be deficient each tonguing exercise can be preceded by a sustained note. When the tongue has learnt to work freely and fast in the lower register exercise must be given to it in the clarinet and high registers. Then the registers should be linked, first by practising a specific number of repeated notes on each degree of an arpeggio and then on each degree of a scale. If the metronome is used and moved up a tick every day this provides an excellent pusher-on of speed.

## SYNCHRONIZATION OF TONGUE WITH FINGERS

When a good speed of tonguing has been worked up on repeated notes, finger work is added. The success of this depends on perfect synchronization between tongue and fingers. First it is necessary to ensure absolute evenness of fingering by practising the passage legato. Then the speed of the tongue is gauged from the *distance between the first two notes* of the passage, and tried out on the initial note only. And finally the two are joined.

## MORE FAULTS

In prolonged staccato playing, especially at only a moderate pace, the pupil often develops noticeable extraneous movement in cheeks, chest or diaphragm. This means he is not keeping up a reserve of air behind the tongue and is pumping from below in spasms. The fault is hard to remove and the teacher will need much patience in eradicating it. If the pupil complains of strain in the throat after practising tonguing this means he is tightening and must be warned to keep it relaxed and well open. If the pupil's reed becomes frayed on the tip this means his tongue is going across the top of it instead of making contact just below. Articulation in the clarinet and higher registers is often accompanied by an undertone. This means that the embouchure is not tight enough and it is probable that the pupil is dropping his jaw with each tongue movement.

## FLUTTER-TONGUING

Flutter-tonguing is an effect demanded occasionally by composers and is a necessary adjunct to the clarinettist's technique.

It is indicated by '*fl* ᴧᴧᴧᴧ ' and is produced not by touch ing the reed but by fluttering the tongue against the roof of the mouth as if rolling an *r*. More of the tongue is wanted for the movement than in normal articulation and so the consonant *d* is used to start it. Again contrary to normal articulation, the jaw is required to drop momentarily and so the consonant is followed by a short vowel which brings it up again into the roll. The pupil should practise first without his clarinet; he starts with the tongue on the roof of his mouth and then withdraws it as if pronouncing *dŭrr* ᴧᴧᴧᴧ.

### TONGUING INDICATIONS IN MUSIC

The term 'phrasing' applied to wind music is synonymous with tonguing and should not be confused with the word's meaning in regard to musical sentences. (The latter is dealt with in Chapter 10.) All indications relating to tonguing have a very exact meaning and it is important for the teacher to be thoroughly conversant with them. Much editing of published wind music has been done by persons not having the necessary knowledge, and this means that the teacher must go through all parts and alter them where markings are misleading or incorrect before giving them to pupils. The following are the basic principles that he will need to know for this:

1. A slur over a series of notes indicates that the first note only is to be tongued, the others to follow on without a break in the continuity of sound.

2. A slur must finish on the note previous to the one next to be tongued.

3. A slur must not be interrupted for a tie but taken over the top of it.

4. A tied note at the beginning or end of a slur must be truly

within it; that is to say, the slur must include all notes of the tie.

5. There should be no slur over repeated notes otherwise this may be read as a tie.

6. A slur ending with a dot indicates that the tongue is to curtail the final note.

7. A single note or series of notes with no indication of any kind means that each note is to be articulated and given its full value.

The latter is called *legato* tonguing, for the tongue does not stop on the reed between notes and no perceptible break is made in the sound. All notes which are to have less than their full value *must* have an indication of the amount of curtailment to be made. Thus the true *staccato*, where the note is to be stopped at half its value, is shown with a dot. The *mezzo-staccato*, where the note is to be given three-quarters of its value, is indicated by a dot and a horizontal line; a series of such notes is given dots and a slur over the top. *Staccatissimo*, the superlative, has its note curtailed at a quarter of its value and is shown with a vertical dash. *But*—and this is where unskilled editors slip up badly—Baroque composers used the vertical dash for *any* note to be tongued, irrespective of the amount of curtailment. They even used it to indicate the beginning of a slur! Only considerable experience can guide the teacher should he himself attempt this kind of editing and he is strongly advised to play the work in question many many times and not to give it to a pupil until he is quite convinced of his decisions over tonguing.

# 8
# *Fingers*

The basis of good finger technique is the *economical* use of the fingers. Natural instincts tend to send the pupil in the opposite direction and he wastes energy. In exuberance he moves his fingers wildly, and when choosing fingerings selects those which occur first to his mind but which may involve more finger movement than is necessary. The teacher's task is to guide him in controlling his fingers and in selecting fingerings for their muscular economy. He must include in his teaching help on the balancing of the instrument, use of the wrists and exercising of the fingers. As Carl Baermann said, "The foundations of technique, as of everything else, have to be laid with care and perseverance."

## BALANCE OF INSTRUMENT

The teacher should first ensure that the instrument has been assembled correctly at the centre joint, because alignment of holes is important to balance. The right thumb is then carefully placed under the rest, along lines suggested in Chapter 4, and when the clarinet is put in the mouth the balance should be correct. The beginner may well experience unsteadiness in this position; if so, he should place his little fingers on their keys to correct it. On no account should he rest the right hand on the bar of the lower joint, which is suggested by some tutors, for this removes the hand from the playing position.

Both hands must be kept in the playing position—over the instrument all the time and the wrists never allowed to sag. The arms should be kept free from the sides of the body otherwise the wrists and thence the fingers are put under strain. The placing of the right thumb under the rest does impose a certain restriction on the hand and if, after a reasonable time of playing, the pupil feels his hand to be in the *wrong* position it may be advisable to try another. A lower position can be sampled by sticking a thick piece of cork or felt underneath the rest. A higher position by unscrewing the rest and placing it the other way round on the instrument. However, only if a really marked improvement in comfort results from one of these tests should the drastic step of drilling fresh screw holes for a new position of the thumb-rest be taken.

## WRISTS

Flexibility of wrists is essential to the movement of the hands and fingers. In the normal hand position the wrists are turned towards the little fingers to enable the latter to be held well over their keys. The position also avoids the accidental touching of break and side keys. When break or side keys are to be used the wrists take the hands over to the keys and return them to the normal position immediately after. If the wrists are not used in these operations the fingers have to be taken to the keys with a rigid hand and forearm and this upsets the balance of the instrument, causing a break in the sound.

## PLACING OF FINGERS

Little fingers should be placed well on to the touchpieces of their keys. When not in use they should remain close over the keys. Often they can be left down in passages around the break and this greatly assists balance. If the pupil has difficulty keeping them where they should be, rubber bands can be brought up over the bell of the instrument, fixed on to key-work and then, with a twist round the tip of each little finger, looped over in such a way as to keep them in place without preventing movement.

All other fingers and the left thumb must, as explained in Chapter 4, be placed over the rings as well as holes, with the pad and not the tip on the hole. The stretch when covering all holes at once is considerable, especially for a child's hand. But the strain which this imposes on the muscles between the fingers is eased if the little fingers are always held well out and close to their keys. The pupil must be given the opportunity to see the teacher's hands in a good position on his instrument, and at home he should practise long notes in front of a mirror to check that he is himself achieving this position.

Under normal conditions little pressure should be used in covering holes. If there is too much, speed is hampered and the balance of the instrument upset when the fingers are lifted for such notes as g′ and c‴. There is a particular tendency to exert finger pressure on high notes, in sympathy with a tight embouchure. To counteract this the pupil should practise soft long notes in this register and try to release the finger pressure. The pressure of the left thumb needs very careful regulation. It must be enough to keep the speaker key fully open and close the hole, and yet not so much as to push the instrument upwards. The pupil should practise long notes on c‴ to find the correct pressure.

### FINGER ACTION

Each little finger has four keys to operate and must move

freely at all joints, especially the knuckles, to do this. Some exercising in this flexibility should be given to the pupil in the form of the following exercises:

1. With all finger and thumb holes closed, each little finger in turn is taken round its four keys, without blowing, first in a clockwise direction and then anti-clockwise. The little finger will move more freely if the ring finger is anchored rather more firmly than usual on its hole. If the pupil has difficulty in this the teacher should help by holding the ring finger in position.
2. The same, but blowing.

Other fingers and the left thumb should lift smartly and half an inch only from their holes. When lifted the thumb must remain under its hole and not stray down on to the woodwork, for this will delay its return to the hole.

### SCALES AND ARPEGGIOS

Fingering is learnt and assimilated in the practice of scales and arpeggios. These should first be taught without music, the teacher writing out the letters only so that the pupil can concentrate on his fingering. If the pupil is familiar with the piano he may be found trying to learn his scales and arpeggios with a keyboard in mind. This method is not successful because the piano repeats its fingering at the octave whereas the clarinet does not, and it should be discouraged. If stimulation is needed in the performance of scales and arpeggios the teacher can bring interest by harmonizing an accompaniment to them. When all scales and arpeggios have been learnt without music, they should be practised with music, so that the pupil becomes familiar with their appearance and will recognize them in his pieces. Tutors come in a wide range and the teacher should select one for the beginner or slow pupil which treats scales and arpeggios from key-note to key-note in a limited compass. The progressive pupil is best served by a tutor that uses the whole compass of the instrument for all keys. The complete coverage needed for the really advanced pupil is not easy to find for many standard books omit such important items as harmonic minors, whole tone scales and augmented triad arpeggios, all of which are essential to his technical equipment. If these items are not in his tutor they must be written out by hand for him to practise.

### DIGITAL EXERCISE

To build up a fluent technique the digits must be exercised energetically and regularly. The basis of this kind of exercise is the trill, or one-finger oscillation. To keep a good balance of the instrument and uniformity of trill, movement should be confined to the finger joints only and kept minimal. It is possible to do some trills quite effectively with a wrist or forearm movement but this is not recommended as it increases muscular effort. Trills should be practised rhythmically, with a definite number of oscillations per beat, first at a slow speed and then at gradually faster ones. In order to encompass all possible finger combinations it is suggested that the trills be performed first on the chromatic scale sequence, then on both whole tone scale sequences and finally on all major and minor scales. As not all fingers are equally tractable the weaker ones must be given extra attention in order to make the technique even. The weakest finger is the ring finger and next to it the little finger. The reason for their weakness is that they are less used in everyday life and this results in the muscle between them being under-developed. This muscle must be strengthened by *keeping the little finger down* whilst working the ring finger hard in the following trills: g♯ to a (d″♯ to e″) and c′♯ to d′ (g″♯ to a″). Trills from the little fingers must also be given extra practice to get them up to standard. It is not advisable to use alternate fingers to help a sluggish little finger trill, as some tutors suggest, because this brings more muscles into play and therefore increases effort.

A few general pointers on trills may be helpful here :

1. To give the trill hand maximum freedom the other hand should take support of the instrument. (This is the only time the left hand does carry the weight.)
2. To give the trill finger maximum freedom the finger next above it should be firmed on its hole.
3. To steady the instrument in trills to or from break keys the left ring finger can be placed on its hole.
4. In a trill from a hole the finger should lift its normal half inch.
5. In a trill from a key the finger should remain in contact with the key all through the movement.
6. In a trill from a fingering normally involving the raising of a key plus the lifting of a finger from its hole, the key can and should be left down for this does not affect the pitch and halves the amount of muscle energy used.

Some of the more unusual trill fingerings need care because their intonation is faulty. These should be practised slowly, giving help to the faulty note with the embouchure. In many trills one or other note may appear to predominate. The pupil should cultivate equality between the sounds by practising the following exercise where the weak note, played first, is given extra strength and length. The exercise should be counted in quavers and strict time kept throughout.

When a thorough mastery of 2-note exercises (trills) has been achieved the pupil should go on to 3-note, 4-note and 5-note exercises. Like trills these exercises should be played in all types of scale sequence, using each successive note as a starting point. They should be played in a group going up, a group going down, and a group going both up and down, i.e. :

## STUDIES

In tackling finger-work studies it is essential that all fingerings where there may be doubt or which deviate from the normal should be marked beforehand, otherwise confusion will arise when they are reached and the fingers begin to 'knit'. When the teacher is presenting a new fingering it is best to give the pupil a diagram or a good description. A demonstration is not easy for the pupil to interpret because he sees it the wrong way round, as if in a mirror.

### LITTLE FINGER KEYS

Duplicate little finger keys are difficult for the pupil to orientate because the layout for each hand is dissimilar. To help identification (and afford innocent amusement to the youngest) coloured paper tabs, bought from a stationer, can be stuck on to the keys, a different colour for each pair of duplicates. Long notes, putting each pair of duplicate keys down together, give the pupil plenty of time to think where the keys are. In guiding him over the choice of little finger keys the following rules should be observed :

1. The left hand e/b″ key, because it lies more naturally under the hand, is used in all scale passages where there is no g♯ or d″♯. When there is a g♯ or d″♯ in the key the right hand duplicate has to be used instead.

2. The right hand f/c″ key, again because it lies more naturally, is used in *all* scale passages where these notes occur.

3. The left little finger should be used in arpeggios where the next note up does not involve lifting other fingers. Where other fingers do have to be lifted the right little finger should be used, so that movement is kept to one hand. This reduces muscle energy and avoids difficult co-ordination between hands. (It will be found that the left hand f♯/c″♯ key is never used in common chord arpeggios.)

4. Where it is not possible to use alternate little fingers a slide between keys must be made. This should be done by keeping the sliding finger light and the ring finger rather more firmly on its hole than usual so that it does not uncover. The most suitable keys to slide from are the g♯/d″♯ and c′♯/g″♯, because the movement involved is outward or downward, which is relatively easy. Slides from other keys involve pulling the finger inward or upward, which requires greater muscular effort.

5. Any of the little finger keys can be used to help bring up the pitch of very high notes. Choice between them will depend not only on the note itself but on the particular instrument, so that it is largely a question of trying them out. In a series of very high notes it is often found that one key will be suitable for the whole sequence and there is no need to change.

FURTHER ALTERNATIVE FINGERINGS

There are many different fingerings for the very high notes on the clarinet. In selecting from a fingering chart it is advisable to use those with less holes covered for scales, as these are quicker to find, and those with more holes covered for arpeggios and sustained notes, where more security is required.

Of the several fingerings for $e'\flat$ and $b''\flat$, the first side key should be used on all occasions except the following :

1. If the notes before *and* after are higher up the instrument, the left ring finger key is used instead.

2. If the notes before *and* after involve the use of the right hand, one or other of the following 'long' fingerings should be chosen according to context :

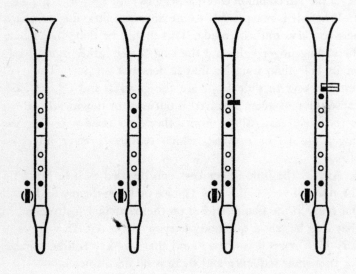

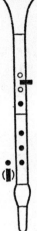

Swopping fingers should be avoided because this is liable to cause a break in the sound. Therefore in moving from b♭ to b♮ or f″♮ to f″♯ the second note should be 'fork' fingered, thus :

Similarly, in moving from f′♮ to f′♯ the second note should be fingered thus :

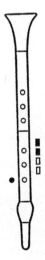

Finally, where a fast passage rises by only a tone or semitone into a higher register the passage should be kept in the lower register by using side or break keys (as in a trill) for the note in question. This secures economy and ease of movement and at the same time speed.

# 9
## *Rhythm*

J. G. H. Backofen tells us in *Anweisung zur Klarinette* (Leipzig 1803) that "of all difficulties the musical scholar has to overcome the greatest is the learning and most exact understanding of time spaces". His choice of the words "time spaces" rather than "time patterns" is all-important and gives us the clue to the whole problem, for there is no dimensional basis to rhythm unless the time of arrival at the next beat is known before departure. Whilst a time pattern can be played correctly in itself, if its speed causes a shortening or lengthening of the allotted time space it is unacceptable and we might join with Shakespeare in saying, "How sour sweet music is, when time is broke, and no proportion kept!"

### SUSTAINED SOUNDS

It will be remembered that in the basic method set out in Chapter 4 the pupil, as soon as he was able to produce a sustained sound, was introduced to a note of definite *duration*, the semibreve, and then to a rest of the same. For both he was taught to start *and finish* at a given moment and here we have the all-important time space. The teacher should continue the doctrine of time spaces in sound and silence with the minim and dotted minim notes and rests. Only after these have been learnt should he tackle the crotchet and sub-divisions of the beat. It will be remembered also that in his first lesson the pupil had to tap out the beats with his foot. This should be continued, in default of a metronome, for his early rhythmic instruction, because he cannot count aloud as he blows and so his foot is his personal time-keeper. He must realize, though, that this is strictly for when he is practising, and never to be done in company. It is important too that his foot movement is kept small and not allowed to affect the rest of his body.

## THE METRONOME

Foot-tapping indicates the player's own idea of the beat and unfortunately this is fallible. Stability in this must be acquired and can only be done by practising with a mechanical beat. The teacher should therefore recommend the pupil to buy a metronome as soon as he can, stipulating that it is the model with a bell. Without this adjunct to show the strong beats the pupil can shorten or lengthen bars without being aware of it. The pupil should use his metronome constantly in conjunction with foot-tapping and in time will acquire a disciplined beat. The metronome is invaluable as a driving power in technical practice and, when gradually moved up, as a pusher-on of speed.

## STRONG AND WEAK BEATS

When the teacher thinks fit to introduce the crotchet he should combine this with instruction on strong and weak beats. The pupil should be given simple melodies, basically in crotchets and with a crotchet time signature, to play with accents at the beginning of every bar. Here the bell of the metronome is particularly useful as the pupil has a constant reminder to accent as it rings. Accents are the beginning of a feel for rhythmic impulse. This should be stimulated further by giving the pupil short exercises in which an anacrusis leads to an accented sustained note, as for instance :

## SUB-DIVISION OF BEATS

The first sub-division to be learnt is the quaver. It is advisable here for the pupil to use his foot and not the metronome to keep time, for in playing two quavers to a crotchet beat the pupil will find the foot's up-movement most useful in timing the second quaver. As the foot's instinct is to go down with a tongue stroke this should be allowed in the early exercises and the first quaver tongued, the second slurred. Later, the foot's independence must be trained by tonguing off the beat. Reliability of the foot with regard to steadiness of beat and independence of fingers and tongue is so important that the pupil must be given plenty of training in it. The trained foot, able to carry on regardless, is the only means whereby he can come to grips with difficult rhythms. Untrained, the foot will stop dead at rhythmic complications or off-beat tonguing and the pupil founders.

When the foot is reasonably safe semi-quavers can be learnt and then the triplet. In the triplet there is a tendency to play the first two notes too close together and it becomes distorted to ♫. . To help spread the notes evenly through the time space an analogy such as 'go to the *beat*' for ♩♩♩ | ♩ might be used. Word analogies are useful aids to the aural appreciation of time patterns. In seeking them the teacher should remember that a second beat must be included in the time pattern otherwise the time space cannot be properly gauged nor rhythmic impulse felt. An isolated time pattern is static, whereas a time pattern within a time space is progressive. The following are examples of suitable analogies :

"Lots to *do*"

"To *town*"

"*A*msterdam, *A*msterdam"

### RESTS

The teacher should ensure that rests, or time patterns of silence, are given as much care as notes. There is much careless rhythm amongst wind players and a great deal of this is due to slackness over rests. Because a breath is usually taken at a rest the tendency is to relax everything, including sense of time. The teacher must insist on no relaxation of time during rests and should give the pupil plenty of exercises to include time patterns of silence between sequences of notes. The metronome should be used for these exercises as it provides an excellent deterrent to slackness.

### DIFFICULTIES

The pupil who hurries a tied note should practise the passage without the tie, when the full value of the note is better understood. In the same way, if a pupil hurries a dotted note, it should be written out with a tied note substituted for the dot and then played as above, disregarding the tie. When a pupil hurries a long note which comes after a sequence of fast ones, he must practise continuing to think in terms of the fast notes during the playing of the long one. This kind of sub-division in the mind should be practised in exercises such as the following:

1. Pupil plays ⟶
   and thinks ⟶

2. Pupil plays ⟶
   and thinks ⟶

If the pupil slows down on fast notes after a sustained note this means he is technically unable to keep the pace and a more suitable speed must be set for the whole.

Beat sense is frequently lost in prolonged passages of fast notes of equal value. The cause of this is a lack of shape in the form of accents, or 'musical lifebelts'. To encourage a feel of the importance of first notes of beats the pupil should practise scales and arpeggios giving greater value than the norm to the first note. Rhythms such as the following might be used for this:

1.                           2.

There are many ways of solving rhythmical problems and the resources available will provide endless stimulus to the enterprising teacher.

### RHYTHM SHIRKERS

Teachers are continually being harassed by certain types of rhythm-shirking pupils. First there are those who say "I shall be able to keep time if you play it with me" or "It went all right when I played it with so-and-so". Then there are those who assert there is no such thing as a metronomic beat in a thing so 'free' as music and in fact have a complete taboo against the metronome. Those in the first category are easier to treat for they do confess to the need for a beat, although relying on someone else to supply it and absolving themselves from any effort in maintaining it. The second category denies the necessity of a beat altogether. Both are musical misfits who spoil the pleasure of anyone they play with. The sadist might put them to play together and wait until total bewilderment set in and showed them the error of their ways. The non-sadist will point out to the first category the necessity for his taking a share in the upholding of the time, and will make him capable of doing it by much practice on his own, with the metronome always going. To the second category he will point out that, except in compositions which are intended to be improvisatory, *rubato* or diversification of time must take place within a certain time space and that this time space is governed by a pre-determined beat. In other words, when he has learnt to *keep* time, then only can he *diversify* time. (See next chapter.)

# 10

# *Interpretation*

Interpretation purports to reveal the meaning. Knowledge of the language involved is implied and obligatory, and where the subject is music, notes are synonymous with letters and time patterns with words. To make words intelligible they must be formed into sentences and expressively narrated. To carry interpretation to its fullest meaning each sentence must be considered as a shape complete in itself yet forming part of the total conception. So : the clarinet pupil now has his vocabulary, the teacher's next task is twofold—to guide in *finding* the sentences and to show how to *present* them, both as entities and as part of a whole creation.

## SENTENCES

Sentences in music are similar to those in the written word and can be split into smaller sections or phrases, each requiring some form of punctuation at the end. Punctuation produces a 'fall of voice' to a greater or lesser degree and its equivalent in music is the cadence. Phrase lengths vary considerably, but in music of the simplest form they are of four-bar duration, each new phrase beginning at the same point in the bar as the first, so that this pattern once started is easy to follow. Practice with uniform phrases first will develop instinct in the pupil which will later guide him in the detection of uneven phrase lengths.

## PUNCTUATION

In wind music as in speech breath is taken at the end of a phrase and Iwan Müller says in his *Anweisung zu der neuen Clarinette* (Leipzig 1826): "The art of taking breath in the right place is uncommonly important. When it is not possessed or wrongly employed this can certainly cause the effect of a piece to be completely missed. It will be chiefly noticeable in passages which have to be delivered with animation, fire and without pause, when the listeners will believe he lacks delivery and taste." To develop this feeling for phrasing which is so important it is advisable for the teacher to mark all breathing places (i.e. cadences) with a tick or comma before the study of a piece is commenced. If phrases are long they should be subdivided appropriately for extra breaths. This can be done at the end of a sustained or tied note, or after a curtailed note such as that at the beginning of a syncopation.

## BEGINNINGS AND ENDINGS

Before expression of the sentence as a whole is considered some help should be given on shaping sentence beginnings and endings. The pupil needs first and foremost to practise the sensitive start required at an anacrusis; this is a refinement hard to achieve for any wind player, the tongue too often producing an accent where none should exist. And he needs to be told that weak endings on unaccented beats or parts of beats should be dynamically tapered off and finished *short* of the following beat, whereas strong endings on accented beats of the bar must be held full length *over to the beginning* of the next beat.

## DYNAMICS

Musical expression is of two kinds: dynamic and rhythmic. The dynamic forces at the command of the clarinettist are greater than on any other wind instrument; however, in proportioning the louds and softs he must bear in mind that his instrument is naturally softer in its low notes and louder on its high than the norm. This is a characteristic which needs to be tempered before a balanced expression can be achieved. To practise this the pupil should be given descending scales on a crescendo and ascending scales on a decrescendo. For a carefully graded change from soft to loud and vice versa long notes on crescendos and decrescendos should be given. A sudden change of expression in music, as in speech, is greatly enhanced and in fact made easier if a breath is taken immediately before it. On all instruments extremes of expression need great care. The value of a true *pianissimo* cannot be overestimated, but it must be so produced that the tone retains its resonance. In *fortissimo* playing on the clarinet, if the blowing is too strong the lips either cannot hold the pressure and there is an escape of air from around the mouth, or the straining of the lips to contain the pressure causes the tone to become hard.

## RUBATO

Rhythmic expression, or *rubato*, should not be frowned upon but practised deliberately, albeit not before the pupil's technique and sense of time have been adequately developed, otherwise the result will be caricature. It is advisable before either an *accelerando* or *ritardando* are made to ensure the pupil is *capable* of going fast enough and to make him practise the whole of the passage at the fastest speed required. This is of especial help in the case of *accelerando*, which is much harder to achieve than *ritardando*. Preliminary exercises for *rubato* should take the form first of trills, then scales and arpeggios, on *accelerando*, *ritardando*, and both. Changes of speed should then be practised within the confines of a phrase, a bar, and a beat.

## CONCEPTION OF THE WHOLE

All expression is conditional and when a pupil can shape an individual sentence artistically he must be taught to fit the sentence into the piece as a whole. Marks of expression are limited and all *fortes* are not equally loud nor *pianos* equally soft, etc. The student-performer must be shown how to discover from the music the relative importance of louds and softs, quickenings and slowings, climaxes and anti-climaxes. Some minutes spent studying the printed page without playing will give the most exact appreciation of the music's general structure.

## CHARACTER

When all this has been done, before performance can take place, the *character* of the piece must be assessed. The composer can only hint at how the music should be played by giving descriptive directions and marks of tempo, the rest must be done by the performer and the teacher may need to bring his histrionic powers into play to stimulate the would-be performer's imagination. Appropriate adjectives can and should be used by the teacher to help evoke the mood or moods of a piece, though he is unlikely to go so far as the pupil who suggested the term *con anima* meant "soggily"!

## PRACTISING

To develop the pupil's imagination and give him practice in diversity of style the many sets of variations written by clarinet virtuosi of the past are most useful. For general control in the shaping of an extended melodic line the slow movements of Spohr concerti offer excellent practice material. To achieve complete dynamic and rhythmic emancipation the student must play cadenzas, and here *Cadenzas, how to phrase them* by Gustave Langenus\* is invaluable. Though expression must be planned and practised yet must it be free within this discipline at performance. To accustom the pupil to this the teacher must give him plenty of opportunities to perform *in the music room*, before ever he is called upon to go out on the platform.

\* Published by **Carl Fischer.**

# 11

# *Ornamentation*

Composers began to write seriously for the clarinet in the 1740s when Baroque ornamentation was flourishing, but by the time the first major works for it appeared, i.e. Mozart's quintet of 1789 and concerto of 1791, the vogue for ornamentation was dying. Until quite recently the tendency has been to regard the clarinet repertoire as beginning with these compositions of Mozart, and so clarinettists have taken the view that they do not seriously require to study ornamentation. However, the discovery and re-publication in recent years of clarinet works of value from the Baroque period make it imperative now for embellishments to be on the curriculum.

## VANDERHAGEN'S GUIDE

The few ornaments still being used by composers today are not all interpreted as they were in the past and to obtain a reliable knowledge of Baroque ornamentation it is very necessary to consult a tutor of the period. It is fortunate that the first clarinet tutor of importance, Vanderhagen's *Méthode nouvelle et raisonnée pour la Clarinette* (Paris 1785), was written just in time to be of use to us in this respect. Vanderhagen describes five essential ornaments in the following manner :

## 1. *The Portamento*

The portamento is an ornament that is added or often found between two notes ascending diatonically. Portamento is a repetition of the first note and should always be slurred to the note that follows.

Value and Interpretation :

EXAMPLE :

Similarly :

## 2. *The Changing Note*

The changing note is also an ornament that is found or some-times added at the end of a bar to make a melody more pleas-ing; the changing note is usually made with a diatonic step or even a third above the one after which it is to be heard. It serves to distinguish and to unite at the same time the inter-pretation of the note which precedes it with the one that follows. As regards the strength to give it, it should be sounded as imperceptibly as if it were the continuation of a sustained note.

EXAMPLE :

It is as well to observe that none of these examples has a fixed speed. They can be played fast or slow as wanted. Many speeds could be given to the same example.

## 3. *Appoggiaturas*

When a small note (appoggiatura) is found in front of a principal melody note this small note should in every case be slurred to the principal note. Appoggiaturas are used in different instances, but mainly if descending in thirds when the intervals are filled in with small notes. Good taste often adds this ornament although nothing is indicated by the writers; there are however instances when one should add nothing, such as in a full orchestral tutti when all the instruments ascend or descend at the same time, for example :

and other similar cases where one should play solely and simply the written notes. Appoggiaturas should only be used for the phrases of a melodic part and above all only when one is alone on the part, because two instruments playing the same part can differ greatly. Their mode of expression being different a bad effect is created straight away. In this case it is necessary to avoid what we call 'embellishing', in other words to add nothing and keep scrupulously to the written note.

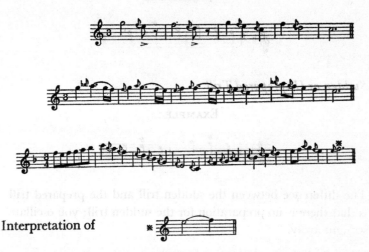

Interpretation of

The interpretation at ✳ is generally used at the end of a melody, holding the little note for two beats and decreasing the sound on it.

### 4. *Trills*

The trill is a rapid agitation of one or two fingers to produce an even and well-sustained oscillation; the trill should last only for the value of the trill note itself. The trill is made by borrowing a diatonic note above that on which one wants to trill; this borrowed note is major or minor according to the mode one is in. When the trill is long the finger movement should be hurried towards the end and terminated briskly.

*The Prepared Trill.* To prepare a trill is to wait a short time on the borrowed note before oscillating.

### EXAMPLE:

## Sudden or Unprepared Trill

### EXAMPLE:

The difference between the sudden trill and the prepared trill is that there is no preparation for the sudden trill; you oscillate straight away.

## 5. *The Mordent*

The mordent is the opposite to the trill as regards the borrowed note. Here it is necessary to borrow the note below the one on which the mordent is written. The trill begins with the borrowed note, the mordent on the contrary begins with the harmony note; but the mordent finishes like the trill, that is with the harmony note.

### EXAMPLE:

Interpretation:

## COMPARISON WITH CONTEMPORARY INTERPRETATION

Vanderhagen's ornaments will now be compared with those in use at the present time. His first two are nowadays generally written into the music and have ceased to exist as ornaments. His third, the true appoggiatura, is common today and played in an identical manner, namely taking half the value of the note on which it leans; if the latter is dotted the appoggiatura then takes two-thirds. But there are important differences in today's interpretation of ornaments 4 and 5. In no. 4, the trill, Vanderhagen begins always on the upper or borrowed note, but since the time of Mozart and Haydn the trill has begun on the written or harmony note. In the case of no. 5, the mordent, Vanderhagen in fact trills to a lower auxiliary for half the value of the note, whereas the modern variant goes to an upper auxiliary, and only once. Nowadays, if a lower auxiliary is wanted the mordent sign has a cross stroke and is designated 'lower mordent'.

## THE TURN AND ACCIACCATURA

Vanderhagen made one surprising omission: he left out the turn. In his time turns were commonplace—they were fitted in almost anywhere—so that he probably considered it superfluous to mention them. The omission is of no consequence, for the turn was the same in the eighteenth century as it is today, and consisted of the note above, the note itself, the note below and the note itself. Another apparent omission is the acciaccatura or short appoggiatura. The probable reason for this omission was that in Vanderhagen's day it was an unusual ornament, and as it was indicated in the same way as the long appoggiatura he preferred to ignore it. Since the nineteenth century the acciaccatura has been shown as a small quaver with a cross stroke. It should be played immediately before the beat.

## PRACTISING

Before the pupil studies a piece of ornamented music he should play it through first without embellishment, to establish the fundamental rhythm in his mind. If the ornamentation is complicated then it is advisable for the teacher to write the music out with the ornaments included to assist the pupil's understanding. A few of the editions of Baroque clarinet music which are on the market today include both ornamented and unornamented versions of the solo part and these make useful studies for the novice. In the playing of fast ornaments such as trills, mordents and acciaccaturas trill fingerings should be used for the auxiliary notes, to obtain maximum speed. Every trill should end on the principal note, except if the following note is the same as the principal note, when it should end on the upper note. In a sequence of trills it is usual to give the final one a turn at the end. If the trill resolves upwards the turn generally takes the form of two notes: the note below and the note itself. If it resolves to the note below, then one note: the note below.

## FAULTS AND DIFFICULTIES

The teacher needs to watch for three common faults at the end of trills:

1. Not keeping the finger needed for a resolution downwards held out in position.
2. Not allowing enough time for the covering of a hole when a downward resolution requires this.

3. Hesitation or slowing down before the resolution when there is no turn.

Double grace notes and mordents are often confused in performance if not in theory; the former, written as two small notes ('shrimps', as a pupil aptly named them) in front of a principal note, is performed with the accent coming on the principal note, whereas the mordent is played with the accent on its initial note. Double grace notes are easier than mordents and should be given to the pupil to practise first. There is a tendency to miss the first note of a fast ornament, where this is tongued. This fault is a combination of sluggish tonguing and not giving long enough to the note for it to speak.

## SUMMARY

Vanderhagen's ornaments, plus the turn and the acciaccatura, provide the necessary basis for the pupil's instruction. If the teacher wishes to study the subject of Baroque ornamentation further he should consult the writings of C. P. E. Bach and of Quantz. He will find many more instances of the Baroque interpretation of an ornament being different to that of the present day, in these writings.

## 12

# *Sight Reading and Transposition*

Both sight reading and transposition are fine sharpeners of
the musical wit and the earlier they are taught the better.
Sight reading should be a part of every lesson just so soon as
the pupil has any musical experience behind him. Transposition, the more difficult art, will of necessity come later,
but must be taught well in advance of the pupil's first orchestral playing.

### DISCIPLINE FOR SIGHT READING

Sight reading is needed not only for orchestral playing but as
an aid to the learning of new music. The pupil who is given
'unseens' regularly will be much quicker at learning his pieces;
he will be able to grasp what the music is about more easily
because his experience is wider. The music chosen for a sight
reading test should be of an easier standard than that of pieces
being currently studied and the teacher should show the pupil
how to get the essence of it before he starts. As a basic discipline, with the test in front of him, the pupil is trained to discover the key, then the time, and to scan it through for any
points of special importance. The pupil's natural instinct is
to worry more about notes than time and he must be told
that rhythm has priority. His final discipline therefore is to
plot the time patterns in the first two or three bars. He is then
ready to start and must play through from beginning to end
without stopping. The point about not stopping must be in-

sisted on, even in the pupil's early stages. Success in this is dependant on looking ahead and if the pupil is trained to do this in all music he plays (see Chapter 2 for method of helping this) he will be the better performer.

## SUGGESTIONS FOR PRELIMINARY INSTRUCTION

As soon as the basic discipline has become automatic some form of general preliminary instruction should accompany each sight reading test. This will help the pupil to find out more about a new piece of music when he is learning alone. The pupil can for instance be trained to recognize scale and arpeggio passages and so be able to play them as a group rather than note by note. He should be given help with Italian words, for these provide a valuable clue to the speed and character of the music. He may need reminding that accidentals ("accidents", as the famous clarinettist Willman liked to call them) last to the end of the bar, and he may need help gauging the length of a tied note, or deciding which fingering to use in an awkward passage over the break. If he has difficulty keeping the key in mind, his sense of key can be stimulated by playing the appropriate scale and arpeggio through first. It is essential that a post mortem of each sight reading test is held, if the pupil is to learn from his mistakes. These tests are of use to the teacher as well in that they can bring to light weaknesses in the pupil which might otherwise remain hidden, if the pupil is a conscientious practiser.

## KEY SENSE IN TRANSPOSITION

Transposition, or changing the pitch of Doh, apart from its orchestral use, is excellent for developing a sense of key. Those pupils who have had experience playing instruments using other clefs besides the treble have an advantage over the clarinet-only pupils for they do not feel bound by a settled pitch. At the start of transposition the new position of Doh must be fixed in the mind. All notes are then moved into the new position and accidentals altered accordingly. As in sight reading, scales and arpeggios should be thought of in groups rather than individual notes. The pupil's earliest attempt at transposition should be made as easy as possible by using a simple piece that he already knows, so that his ear will tell him when he goes wrong. He should first be given the transposition that he will need most in the orchestra, namely up a tone, as if he were playing a part for clarinet in C. This will stand him in good stead should he be asked, as surplus clarinets often are, to fill in for a missing performer on any other instrument pitched in C. If the pupil does not possess an A clarinet he should also have some practice in transposing parts for the A, down a semitone. In doing this he will not have to change the letter name if the original key has sharps, but he does have to if there are flats.

### SUITABLE MATERIAL

Recorder music makes suitable material for both sight reading and transposition in the early stages and oboe or violin music, provided this does not go too high, works well for the later stages. A stimulus to continuity can be provided by accompanying the pupil on the piano. And likewise, sight reading and transposition in the ensemble class stimulates the players to keep going; here it has a challenging effect and produces a rare sense of pulling-together in a sink or swim atmosphere.

# 13

# *Practice*

## PLANNING

Klosé says, in his *Méthode pour servir à l'enseignement de la clarinette à anneaux mobiles* (Paris 1843): "Regarding the manner of studying—few people reap from their labours the fruit that they expect to; this happens because they have not organized their studies, they have not had a reliable guide to direct them." A well-organized and conscientious teacher will generally proceed with each lesson in the same order and manner in which he expects his pupil to practise. But the fact that he proceeds thus for a reason will not be apparent to the pupil. Left without guidance the latter will go into what interests him most, his music, skipping the technical exercises, and most probably *playing* the music, not practising it. He must have it explained to him that before justice can be done to the music all muscles used in playing need to be exercised, exercised in the right order and the right manner. The order for exercise is: breathing, lips, tongue, fingers. The right manner is set out in the paragraphs below.

The proportions of a properly balanced practice should be roughly as follows: the first quarter of the time allotted, long notes proceeding to tonguing exercises; second quarter, finger exercises, scales and arpeggios; third and fourth quarters, studies proceeding to pieces and sight reading. The teacher should make a point of giving this plan in the early stages of the pupil's training. At every lesson he will give help with practising specific things and will make clear how much he expects the pupil to achieve before the next lesson.

### LONG NOTES AND TONGUING

The objects of long note practice are to achieve control of breathing, to strengthen the lips, and to develop good quality sound with steady intonation. Because the embouchure fares best if firmed up gradually it is advisable to start in the low register and work gradually upwards. The notes of the arpeggio being currently studied could to advantage be used for this, or for a child who is uncertain of his letters an excellent plan is to give long notes on one letter in all (to him) known fingerings until he has mastered them. The object of tonguing exercises is to develop the tongue's strength and speed, and to acquire precision in attack and finish of notes. Routine exercises for this should include staccato sounds stopped by the tongue and separated by rests, and also fast repeated notes with no break between them. Further exercises can be found in Chapter 7.

### FINGER EXERCISES
### SCALES AND ARPEGGIOS

Finger exercises to develop strength, nimbleness and speed should take the form of those suggested in Chapter 8, beginning with single digits and progressing to two, three, etc. In scales and arpeggios, especially when many are being practised for an examination, the pupil should be trained to decide before he starts, which little finger key he is going to use first over the break, for this is a place where indecision occurs. In minor keys he should also visualize the fingering of the sixth and seventh degrees of the scale before starting. Unevenness is likely to occur in scales when crossing the first break going up and the second break coming down and this should be given special attention.

## STUDIES AND PIECES

Learning a new study or piece involves training the memory afresh and if too many notes are tackled at the same time the mind is over-burdened and no clear image formed. The pupil should therefore be advised to learn in small sections and to master each section before going on to the next. Speed is not necessary at the beginning; muscular and mental familiarity will come more easily with slow practice. This will also ensure that no notes are skimped and there will be time to give attention to smoothness of fingering and steadiness of rhythm.

## WAYS TO PRACTISE

The young pupil's instinct is to correct mistakes *en passant*, with the result that they occur again at the lesson. He needs to be shown how to come to grips with the mistake, to practise it on its own many times until it is right and then to fit it into the phrase as a whole. When small sections of phrases are practised they should always be done rhythmically, from the beginning of one beat to the beginning of another beat, never starting or stopping in the middle of a beat. In this way both rhythmical and technical command become greater. If a pupil says a difficult passage does not respond to his practising, even though he has followed his teacher's instructions, then it is obvious that new ways of grappling with the problem must be found. Variations in rhythm or tonguing can often help, a *tenuto* given to a single difficult note can breed confidence, etc. If a phrase fails continually to respond to technical practice, a switch to the study of it from the interpretive angle can relax a muscular tension which was preventing progress, and then the passage can be played quite easily. When a phrase recurs in the same form but in different keys in the same movement, using the easiest version as copy for the others can be a help.

### HOW TO PRACTISE

The pupil should be encouraged to mark his music when necessary during practice, just as the teacher does for him in the lesson. He should play standing as well as sitting, for both are required in different types of performance. It is useful also for him to practise in rooms with different acoustics; for instance, the small 'dead' carpeted room enables him to assess his tone quality more critically, while the large uncarpeted resonant room gives him necessary 'size of performance'. The pupil who practises for considerable periods of time at a stretch, or one who has been playing a quantity of high notes, may complain that the inside of his bottom lip is painful or even cut. If a cigarette paper folded into four thicknesses is moistened and moulded over the bottom front teeth this will act as a buffer to the lip and he will be able to continue playing without further harm. This treatment should be applied as soon as soreness occurs, for to continue with a cut lip can in severe cases cause lasting damage.

# 14
# *Performance and Nerves*

## REASON FOR AND AVOIDANCE OF NERVES

Performance begins at the lesson and ends at the concert. Nerves are a wretched state of mind and body which can spoil that concert if they are not understood and steps taken beforehand to prevent them as far as possible. They are caused by uncertainty and fear of the unknown. Certainty and knowledge must be given to the pupil by the rigorous preparation not only of his music but in the *presentation* of it. In this preparation the teacher must include the following : choice of suitable music, help in memorizing, coaching the pupil with the other performer(s), advice on reed selection and above all instruction on platform procedure and deportment.

## CHOICE OF MUSIC

Choice of music is necessarily influenced by the programme as a whole and by the type of audience, but whatever the requirements the music should be selected if possible from the existing repertoire of the pupil, for this will give him confidence. And he should be allowed to play music which is well within his technical capacity so that he can enjoy his performance. On no account should he perform a piece which is beyond his technique because this will destroy his confidence completely.

H

## MEMORIZING

If the concert piece is to be a solo or concerto it should be committed to memory if possible. Memorizing promotes a much more complete understanding of the music and should form a part of every musician's training. It is most easily done when the music is studied for the first time and impressions on the mind are strongest, but can be done at a later stage if the right instincts have been developed. The young child is often capable of doing it simply on demand and uses mainly his tactile and visual senses. The older pupil, as he becomes progressively more conscious of what he is doing, finds these senses alone let him down. The teacher must now show him how to analyse the music and if this ability is developed so that it is done automatically as each new piece is learnt the pupil will memorize easily. In performing from memory the main danger lies in distraction of the attention; it is therefore advisable for the pupil to get used while practising to resting his eyes on a stationary object in front of him, at eye level, and to do this at performances too.

## PREPARATION FOR ENSEMBLE PLAYING

Before the finished piece is performed with the other player or players the pupil must know something about the rest of the music and how his part fits into it. He is taught to look at the score and discover what happens at vital points such as the opening, at pauses, during rests and changes of time, etc., and to mark his part with cues that will serve as reminders. If the work is complicated and the clarinet part in the score is printed in his own key then the pupil should practise from this, following the other parts at the same time.

## GIVING DIRECTIONS

In ensemble work all directions should be given by visible, not audible means. The two principal movements that the clarinettist needs to give are as follows :

1. Lifting the bell of his instrument from the playing position and returning it smartly for bringing the other players in.
2. Lifting the bell outwards and up for taking them off.

He indicates any variation of speed by giving the down movement on every beat requiring direction. He should get used to giving these movements the first time he plays with his teacher, and should also have practice in taking movements from the teacher whilst playing duets, so that in group work he can take leadership from others.

## FITTING TOGETHER

Ensemble playing requires an attentive ear, together with the realization that a slower moving part must fit with a faster. This often presents a problem to the pupil and some practice along the following lines will help him :

1. Listening to the accompaniment and counting aloud to it, without playing himself.
2. Listening and counting whilst fingering the part on his instrument.
3. Listening and playing the part very softly.

When the pupil can play confidently with the teacher accompanying him he must rehearse with his concert accompanist. Playing with another can be disconcerting to the pupil, for he will miss many things which his teacher, through his peculiar insight into both parts, has been able to give him. The teacher must therefore help with the rehearsing. This should be done frequently and well in advance of the concert. A good start is the first essential, for this will arouse the interest of the audience. Then the teacher should make sure that his pupil is as firm in giving directions as he was when playing with him and that the pianist is responsive in accepting these directions. Interpretation and balance must be guided and then the two players made aware of the importance of a good final note so that the audience remains interested to the end.

### REED CONFIDENCE

Familiarity with a selected reed is the secret of confidence in blowing. The embouchure must be thoroughly used to a reed for certainty of control to ensue. The teacher should therefore advise the pupil to select a concert reed some time in advance and to *use it until the concert.* If not given help with this important matter pupils tend to do one of two unsatisfactory things : they leave selection till much too near the concert, through forgetting about it or a mistaken idea that it is best to have a brand new reed; or they select some time in advance and lay the chosen reed aside, using another one until close on the concert. In both cases the embouchure has not sufficient time to settle down to the chosen reed. In the second case there is an added disadvantage in that as the embouchure had adapted to another reed in the interim the original reed may no longer feel so good as it did.

### WARMING UP

Time must be given before a concert to moistening the reed and blowing it in, as well as warming the instrument up to pitch. It is only too easy for the pupil to become self-conscious about doing it when the time comes or be distracted by other things going on around him. The teacher must train him to regard it as a highly necessary preliminary, for without it his performance is certain to be poor at the start and may never recover.

## PLATFORM PRESENTATION

Presentation on the concert platform is not a natural phenomenon. The unfortunate pupil who goes out onto the platform not knowing what to do, hesitates and evokes no welcome from the audience; shocked, he is attacked by nerves and his permance is ruined before it began. An experience such as this will deter him from any further performance and must not be allowed to happen. The teacher must instruct him in the following platform drill which should be rehearsed many times until it becomes natural behaviour :

1. Walking onto the platform, as far as the playing position, without hesitating and with a cheerful expression.
2. Facing the audience, and then bowing slowly from the waist whilst looking towards the floor.
3. Adjusting the music stand for height and for its position in relation to the other players and the audience.
4. Tuning up.

And for after the performance :

5. Walking off smartly.
6. Coming back to take the applause as for the entrance, and departing as before.

An ensemble must be rehearsed in platform drill too and with all the players present. The one who has to walk farthest to his seat will enter first, followed by the others in order of platform position. When the last player has arrived, all bow together, taking their cue from the first player. At the end of their performance the player who came in last leads the bow and departure from the platform.

## DRESS REHEARSAL

A dress rehearsal under simulated concert conditions is of immense value. Not only will the pupil have a chance to discover his weaknesses in time to put them right before the concert, but, with the teacher there to help him he will learn to cope with the unexpected. No concert goes entirely according to plan and irregularities must not be allowed to upset the performance. The rehearsal is of use to the teacher as well, for he will be able to assess his pupil's potential and examine his general demeanour. Regarding demeanour Henry Lazarus says to his pupils in his *New and Modern Method* (London 1881): "Bear a calm appearance, emit the sounds without showing externally the difficulties that have to be overcome. It will greatly impress those around you with the apparent facility of your execution. On the other hand it would offer the company some temptation to laugh if you were to move your head, balance the body, rise [*sic*] the shoulders as a mark of expression, fill up your cheeks with wind, etc." A mannerism is rarely deliberate, but generally unconscious and the result of tension. It may have lain unnoticed in the lessons, but on the platform becomes pronounced through increased tension. If the mannerism is stopped then so is the pupil's tension.

## PERFORMANCE

The teacher should go to the actual concert if at all possible. His presence is necessary to the pupil in that he alone can give a true valuation of the performance and tell him if he did himself justice. In assessing the performance the teacher should comment fairly, giving constructive as well as critical advice and not omit to offer encouragement for future occasions. He will learn much himself from the concert, for often the pupil then reveals a quite different side to his character. The confident one may in spite of all his training become a victim of nerves, or on the other hand he may do better than his best. The indifferent one may prove himself capable of rising splendidly to the occasion, but if the one who works conscientiously and is technically sound goes to pieces with nerves then he should probably keep off the concert platform. If a naturally nervous pupil is able to disguise his nerves, and if during the experience of future concerts is able to rise above those nerves into inspiration, then the teacher could not ask for a greater reward.

# POSTSCRIPTS

POPULARITY : 13-year-old pupil to clarinet teacher just arrived from England to teach at large public school in Australia : "Say, sir, did the College buy you from England?" "What *do* you mean, Peter?" "Well—you know, like footballers.'"

IF IT HAS TO BE DONE : 10-year-old pupil, on being asked when he would do his practice : "While my foot is in water." "Why, what a funny time to choose, Johnny!" "Well you see, sir, last week I ran 100 yards in 12 seconds and hurt my foot, and as I have to sit with it in water for half an hour that is when I shall do my practice."

WAIT FOR IT : "Now Joan, I want you to play the scale containing all the semitones. What is it called?" "The dramatic scale, sir."

THE DISHONEST ART : "You must give long enough to that ornament, Bettine—it takes half the value from the note it precedes. And what is it's name?" "An apologyura, sir."

(With acknowledgements to George Draper and Paul Harvey.)